LIGHT YOUR SOUL ON FIRE

Living a truly abundant and aligned life.

By
Becca Grabinski

HELLO beautiful SOUL!

Let me introduce myself –

I am a midwestern girl that shifted from a life of 'shoulds', going through the motions, focused on who society says I should be, caring what everyone thinks of me, feeling stuck, unfulfilled, quite lost actually...

TO....

Digging deep inside, searching for my purpose, looking at what REALLY lights me up, redefining life on my terms, deciding that my life gets to ROCK, that I get to be, do, have what I want (not in a materialistic way but what creates a feeling of wholeness within), done with drama, speaking from my soul, serving the people that want the same!

I am not here to survive.

I am here to heal my pain and thrive.

I am here to teach those ready to shift into continual joy, happiness, wholeness, fulfillment from the inside.

You may not like or agree with me. I may trigger you. Know it is always from a place of radiating love.

Welcome to my story. My transformation. I wrote this in the hopes of inspiring you to follow your soul. To trust in your guidance system. To live this life in a way that LIGHTS your soul on fire!

xo

Becca

THIS BOOK was inspired by:

The teachers in my life that have challenged me to think bigger. To allow myself to feel it all. Without you I wouldn't have this story to share and souls to heal.

- ♥ To Curt. You have been instrumental to this process of watching me uncover ALL my crap right in front of you. Constantly fixing, searching, hiring new coaches, and diving SUPER deep into hard and ugly stuff. I commend you for supporting me through this and encouraging me. It means the world.

- ♥ To Tony – Tony Robbins that is. He showed me deep transformation can happen in a moment. That a morning routine that is consistent and powerful to living an incredible life. He has shown me the power of energy in a chill way. You are profound, and I am grateful that you use your talents to change the world.

- ♥ To Kris. When I encountered the bottom of the pit. You were there to coach me. You laid the foundation and stood by me as I took the beginning steps even where there were no stairs to be found. I am forever grateful for your friendship.

- ♥ To Bob Proctor. You helped me understand the mind in a way that seldom teach. That anything is possible. Even though I wanted to believe it – you showed me proof repeatedly.

- ♥ To Amanda Frances. You have rocked my world in letting me be me. To step into my authentic self. To do it my way without rules. It works. It feels so good and my soul is SO happy. The world will see the true me because you gave me the permission, I never knew I needed to step into my light.

- ♥ To Katrina Ruth. You showed me that the ONLY way is soul work. Letting my soul speak every day. Even when it seems jumbled or confusing. That my purpose work is all that matters. Paid or not.

- ♥ To my family. For hearing me and listening to me and allowing me to share my healing with them. Your support means the world and we collectively can help so many that just don't know where to go or what to do.

- ♥ To my kids. For believing in me. For challenging me. For allowing me show up in the world my way and encouraging it. Grateful for your love. Excited to see your souls develop and grow.

Xo.
Becca

Table of Contents

Introduction

The truth is there is SO much more to life than what society lets us in on UNLESS we are paying attention. Cheers to you for deciding to see it. And for allowing yourself to see this thing called life much differently than you do now.

Societal programming and other humans throughout our lives have altered our view of the world. Handed over beliefs about life, success, happiness, peace, relationships, etc. that shape the way we currently see the world. Throw your desire into the mix and as long as the beliefs don't shoot them down - you are on fire. A soul on fire! If the subconscious beliefs do not support the desire it will leave one stuck, doubtful, discouraged, possibly even quitting.

Join me on my journey of 'others' beliefs hindering the joy that is available to all of us. In this beautiful life we are all here to experience it gets to be joyful. It gets to be easy. It gets to be SUPER flow.

By releasing a life of 'shoulds'.

You CAN be, have, and do what you desire. You REALLY can. But gosh that self-doubt can get heavy. Destroying all that you may have in your life and manipulating your life into one of mediocre crap. Really. Allowing us to spend more time looking at what others are doing and then telling a story about why not us. Or why they can, but not us. It is debilitating. Overwhelming. And for SURE discouraging.

"Your desire to change must be great than your desire to stay the same." Unknown

SO how do we work through the ever-loving changes in our world? The perceived good and bad ALL WHILE attempting to make this life great? Good question huh?! Well this book is about debunking the STUFF. The stuff that constantly blocks and alters our view of life. We will go deep and sometime stay in the shallow. We will learn to shift our expectations and make some decisions that will forever alter the trajectory of our lives. Together. Locking arms. Doing the damn thing. AND letting it be easy. You ready?!

Ok great.

You will NOTICE journal prompts throughout this book. They are there for YOU to uncover the subconscious crap lingering in your blind spots. Dive into them. Write whatever comes out. Some of it may surprise you. Know that healing these aspects of you will create space for the amazing life that is meant for YOU! This isn't a one-time gig. I teach processes and ways to look at things – but it is like working out. We need to build the muscle AND THEN maintain. Trust yourself in this process. KNOW that you are exactly where you are supposed to be – and WILL transform your life in the perfect way specific for your necessary growth.

Side note: What you are seeing on the cover is something SUPER meaningful to this entire book. When we feel practically underwater, but we DECIDE that we are going to hold onto what flame we have left in life. We hold it high over our head – EVEN when we can't breathe. There is hope. Hope to fan the flame within. To let it come to the surface. Be ok with wherever your flame is right now and know that you can fan it and it WILL burn brighter once you decide to CHOOSE you above all else.

Yellow on the back cover - signifies the Solar Plexus chakra which is an energy center right above your belly button. Our FIRE for life comes from this energy center. Yellow instills optimism, wisdom, enthusiasm, and joy. When this chakra is blocked, we experience, anger, fear, shame, resentment, hate, and bitterness. When this chakra is balanced, we experience creativity and the feeling of expansiveness to be our authentic self – the one that FEELS the best, most aligned version of ourselves.

What you need to know.

This book is a collection of my personal life experiences along with deep introspection. It starts at a major event that really changed a lot of my life and completely overhauled my life's direction. AND then.... We go backwards. So, hang on tight. Get ready for the ride.

I start out with my beliefs that could have debilitated me and did for a while. I will sometimes end with a re-write. I tell a different story. Do you ever notice when you look at what ACTUALLY happens it is much different than the story you tell? As in you added a bunch of 'stuff' around what you are making it mean. We do that. We define things based on our experiences and perceptions. It really gets us in trouble, and it gets us stuck. On the Ferris wheel and we can't get off.

The re-write looks at the actual and how we can re-frame the way we tell the story to enhance our lives and allow our flame within our soul to brighten a bit more. Strengthening the flicker.

Why this book?

First off. My goal here is to show you that there are NO rules. As in ANYONE can write a book and serve the world. Including YOU. If you have a message that can help at least ONE person. Do it! This book may contain errors etc. It may come off a little hard. Stick with me. As humans our goal is progress never perfection. You will see this in all my work. I show my human self – completely authentic. I self-published to SHOW myself and the world that I don't need a brand, a ghost writer, or anyone really to help me get my message out. AND neither do you. It can block our creative flow. Do it how you flow. Do it authentically. Let it come from you.

Where I was?

You would seriously NOT recognize me 5 years ago. Although I have always been hard driving of myself and using some of these skills we will talk about in this here book – I wasn't doing ANY of it consistently. I also didn't know why or what or how. I was lost. Wondering what in the world I am supposed to be doing and why I feel SO shitty all the time.

I was reacting to everything. I was the victim of life. Empty. I put ALL my energy into making accomplishments my focus. What could I do in this lifetime and speed through it? Hurry up, let's go. Never allowing myself to be in the moment or even know what being present was.

I am grateful for all these lessons and the humans involved in them. Life is a journey and I hope to inspire you to see your world better after reading this book.

Walking Out of the Court Room

Belief: Divorce is painful, damaging and you become a failure.

The musty smell of the courtroom and the uncomfortable stares of those waiting for their turn, listening to my choice to alter my family forever. Don't turn around Becca. Don't make eye contact. Did I just do that? Did I just alter my children's entire life? Am I making the right choice? Did I try hard enough to honor the vows I made 5 years ago? I stepped out of the courtroom, my hands still shaking, trying to hold the tears back, and replaying the entire event. Sitting in front of a judge in a room full of people as your divorce decree is being read out loud, agreeing to every single piece of heartbreak. A vow I said I would never break, an event I said would never happen to me. I did it. The big divorce. I just went through all of this with my parents' divorce. I am not a quitter. The odd feeling of relief. The black cloud was no longer lingering above my head. The toxic life I lived dissolved as the papers were signed. The storm was starting to clear or, so I hoped.

Let's talk about vows. Whatever God has brought together do not separate. I questioned all I was ever taught about what marriage is. What if this was complete free will? We have that ability don't we. Or is this just my way of justifying my guilt? What did I just do?

The numb feeling, I had for days after I gave credit to history repeating itself. I was actually more prepared for this than I would had imagined. The deep pain still piercing my heart. I allowed myself to feel every inch of the choices I was making. I put the dagger in my heart, and it was time I take it out. It didn't come out in one piece. Broken piece after broken piece as I searched internally and addressed my shadows straight up.

Alligator tears hit the wood floor as my mom showed up on my doorstep. I called her in total disarray, and she didn't even hesitate to call into work and drive two hours to be my backbone and shelter my kids from their Mother falling apart. The reality was setting in. I could not function. She brought the kids downstairs as she handed me my phone to call someone to help me through this. I have the best Mom in the world. Seriously!! She has picked me up off the floor every time I crumble, my entire life. I called the first therapist I found that would answer the phone and get me in the same day. What could they possibly do to help my healing?

I mustered up the energy to shower in hopes that the water would wash away the hives that collected on my face. Being dressed and showered helped me to feel a little human. I pulled myself together and drove to the therapist office. I pulled into to this dilapidated strip mall in hopes that this would not be a waste of money. This therapist greeted me. She was extremely young (like 18 years old) and I instantly went to victim mode. What does she know about divorce, young kids, and putting life back together? I leaned back on the leather couch sticking to part of it as I lost a part of myself. Two words to describe how I felt. Empty. Failure.

I slumped into my seat dreading having to talk about the shadows that have been lurking my closet for more of my life than I am comfortable with. She pulled one painful experience after another out of me and set it on the proverbial table sitting between us. She ripped apart my childhood, patterns I was repeating, and wounds I had intentionally chosen to forget about. She didn't own enough tissues in this tiny office for the emotions I was releasing. We needed some serious sage burning. The mental fog was starting to lift slightly. Telling her my life story with all the trials and tribulations brought me to a place of clarity, I thought. It was time to step up and walk across this plank I was so avoiding. The world of fear that I lived in for over 30 years was controlling my every move. I was done. Done with being fearful.

I set my intentions to start living an extraordinary life from here on out. I will start to choose love over fear. It sounds easier than it really is.

Divorce. I told myself it would never be me. I choose to marry because deep down I didn't believe anyone else would marry me. Quick. Hurry! Jump in while I can. Avoid being the lonely cat lady forever. It was all based on fear. Based on the lack of belief in myself. Based on the lack of love for myself. Once married it would never end right? That's what they told me.... I mean it was a substantial upgrade from the last AND an incredible lesson that I will never regret. This divorce was catalyst for living an extraordinary life. It all started with a decision.

The moment when it all made sense. I was happy. Relieved. Free. So why all this pain? Where is it coming from? What created it?

It was staring right in front of me. The loss of a dream.

As a little girl I made photo albums of my wedding day. Every guy I dated I would size him up to see if he fit. I was laser focused on this dream of who this man was. I put this life together perfectly. 4-year degree, great job, meet a guy, get married, buy a house, have 2.5 kids, life happily ever after. That was the dream I painted, and I did it ALL with perfection in a short amount of time. This dream was so ingrained in my bones to watch it fall apart was the hardest part. My pain was completely created from the life I wanted to live to now having to surrender to whatever it is supposed to be.

The story I told myself was not what happened, and I crumbled NOT because it changed but because I was SO fearful of the story looking different than how I planned it. But let's get SUPER REAL. Who has made a 'plan' for their life and it ACTUALLY happened? Nobody. But yet we still continue to plan out our future and then completely self-destruct when it doesn't come to fruition. Interesting huh? It is like laying out our own land mines and then stepping on them and getting upset about it. Let's look at this in a different lens.

It was TIME. Time to trust my inner guidance, BUT I had to ask for what I wanted. No pressure, right?! Manifesting a new life or just surrendering and letting life happen to me. How could I create a picture of what I wanted when the last one crumbled? How do I even KNOW what I want?

Gosh this manifesting thing is SO much easier than the plan. Trusting – this or something better. Without needing to know how. Let this be easy Becca.

"Just believe in yourself. Even if you don't, pretend that you do, at some point you will."
Venus Williams

We all have spiritual abilities. It is trusting the nudge. The voice. The feeling. There is so much judgement around them and what they are. Let them be and TRUST.

Re-write

Divorce was my catalyst for living an extraordinary life. The lessons were profound. I will never 'fail' at another relationship because failure just means that I chose to be a victim. My kids picked up 4 amazing loving people that all guide them and teach them different life lessons. This life is a journey. People are in our lives for a reason, a season, or a lifetime AND it is none of my business which one they are. It is my job to keep my heart open and to be in the moment.
I show up now in relationships with deep love. Boundaries. When I am triggered, I look directly at me instead of blaming the other. When in reality I manifested this divorce. I only looked at the ways in which it wouldn't work. So, the results were, it

didn't work. I am grateful for this lesson and grateful to allow my children to see what a healthy relationship looks like. Divorce is a choice. It is an ending to a lesson and a beginning with a blank notebook that allows you to write the story any... I mean ANY way you wish.

Journal It Out

- Look back on the perceived failures in your life.

- Who have you become because of those events?

- Break them down one by one.

- Why are you grateful to have experienced these events?

- How has your future decisions changed due to this event?

- Where can you see the light instead of the darkness?

Looking for Love

Belief: My joy comes from external sources.

Do you have a person in your life that you have put up so ridiculously high on a pedestal? They can do absolutely no wrong. Looking off into the mountains in my hotel room as I write this, thinking about this amazing person in my life. He could fix anything, and it was always done perfectly, even if it took longer. It always took longer. Way longer. The price paid for perfection. I could go to him for any advice although looking back I should have taken more of it. He had a gentle calmness about him all the time that was comforting to be around. In my eyes he could do no wrong.

It was time. The tears started rolling down my face. Standing in the doorway with the cool breeze blowing in I watched my Dad pull his horn of his beautiful shiny semi to head back to work for the next couple weeks. My heart felt broken. Why was he never here? Why did he have to work so much? My younger self didn't understand. The roar of the truck faded away as I plopped myself down on the stairs and cried until I had no tears left. My Dad was the man I placed high on a pedestal. Every man that came into my life was compared against him and in all honestly nobody could add up. This little girl's heart broke every time that truck pulled out of our dirt driveway. The problem was this man I put up on a pedestal was human. Flawed just like the rest of us. I just didn't know that then.

I did it. I finally graduated from college after 7 years of trying to 'figure out' what direction I wanted to go in my life. I started at a school out of state and picked a major based upon how much money I could make. Oh wait... let's be honest. I picked it because my older amazing sister attended there. My father always spoke so incredibly high of her. If only I could live up to her standards. But I dropped out. Good old college dropout could barely survive the first year. I moved home without telling anyone. Fall rolled around and my mom, with a light step in her foot said cheerfully, "Are you excited to head back to school?" I guess it was time I told her. I am not going back. Her face soaked in disbelief.

All I wanted was approval from my parents. This was surely not going to do it. She quickly turned around and asked what my plan might be. The truth was there was no plan. My depression was at an all-time high. I was as far off my life path as I could get. She wasn't buying it, so I let her choose my next steps. Lucky me she said I should attend cosmetology school. I always cut my Dad and brothers hair and sometimes experimented with color. It was 10 months. What did I have to lose? It was 10 short months of a blessing and being able to live with my amazing Grandma. The days were long but fast. In school 8-5 and serving until midnight to 2 am at the local IHOP. I sure knew my pancakes.

Living with Grandma provided me a bonding that will never dissipate even though she has moved on from this life. Do you ever notice how people are placed on your path right when they are needed? It wasn't a coincidence. She had advice and wisdom for me that I didn't understand then, but it dripped into my future perfectly.

Once I graduated, I was blessed to work at a spa which was beyond heavenly. Finally, some money rolled into my life. Thank you to my brother for finding this great opportunity. The job was incredible, but the management was another story. I ended up leaving due to morals and standing up for myself. One of the first times I started to create some type of boundaries for myself. The beginning of what I didn't know then - self-love.

I was able to talk to many career professionals that visited the spa to finding something that lit me up like no other! Finance! Oh, how I love numbers. Notice I didn't say math. Totally different beast. Who knew spreadsheets and numbers would be so fun for my creative quirky personality? I was finally headed back to college. Ready to check off the societal success box number 2. The school that my Dad said I should have attended right out of the gate while living at home. Remember I never actually took his advice.... Oh yes, let's try college this again! But wait. Let's live as far from campus as I can without making any friends. So, I can for sure succeed! (Another story...)

I had been telling my Dad the date of college graduation for over a year so he for sure would not miss it. As he missed almost everything. At least that is what it felt like. His work schedule had always been sporadic, so he has missed a lot of big events and I was determined that this wasn't going to be one of them. The long hours with my head in a book while still working full time were so worth it. Bachelor of Science. Wow.

I ran to the bookstore to purchase my gown and called Dad. 'Hey - the big day is next week. You are going to be able to make it right?!' A long pause on the other end. 'I will do the best I can.' He muttered like his usual answer. His voice was quiet, and the conversation was over.

I had talked to him almost every single day but today was different. I had this feeling deep in my gut that should have prepared me. The sensation was sickening. I completely choose not to listen or feel it. I just stuffed it and went along with my plan. He will be there. A Dad is 'supposed to' be at the biggest events of their child's life.

I jumped out of bed Saturday morning so ready to walk to get that diploma I worked so hard for. Remember society says that you have made it once you get that degree. My new career was already lined up and I was beyond ready for the next steps. My body was quivering with excitement that I was ready to move onward and upward. I put my best dress on and called my Dad.

My heart sunk for the hundredth time. Please don't tell me you can't make it. I lost it. Literally lost it. My head pressed against my steering wheel and my tears covered my favorite dress. Today is the biggest day of my life. An accomplishment I didn't think would ever come and he is going to miss it. Why am I surprised? I told him hundreds of times when the date and time and location was for over a YEAR. How could he do this to me? My insides felt like shriveling up and hiding in my bed for the day. The rage started to set in. My mom pulled in and didn't say a word. She didn't have to. She has been through this over and over and over again.

She gave me the best mom hug (you know what I mean here) and we headed to the ceremony. I spent the evening in total breakdown and my heart was broken. Lucky for all the amazing people that came to support me. I was a total and utter wreck. How could I forgive him for missing the biggest day of my life? I covered myself in unforgiveness and chose to put a dagger in my heart. Little did I know the only person I was hurting was myself.

After countless years of the absence of this man I started to look for love elsewhere going from boyfriend to boyfriend with little time in between. Triggering hard my feeling of abandonment that played out in ALMOST every relationship I have had.

Trying to fill this void in my heart from someone that was completely human. Flawed like the rest of us. The standards I set for him were completely unrealistic. The expectations I had he could never meet. I started to feel like I NEEDED someone to be whole. I felt SO empty. SO alone. I settled for what I thought I deserved. Looking for love outside of me.

Society says that a Dad 'should' show up in a certain way in a child's life. A Dad 'should' act a certain way. There is a definite definition of a 'good' Dad. Have you ever stopped to question where the definition came from? And WHY most Dad's do not fit well in this description letting down the very kids that held up to this belief?

It started with allowing him to be who he is without having to walk on egg shells to be what everyone else 'thinks' he should be.

Re-write:

My joy is always from within. My relationship that I focus on is with me and me. When I improve me all my relationships improve. Having expectations on how others should live their lives is just a projection of my own truth on others. Beliefs that were really never mine in the first place. Judgement is the opposite of love and acceptance. Everyone is doing the best they can. Everyone gets to decide. Everyone gets to be authentic even when it isn't the way we believe they should be. I choose to love others exactly where they are at AND honor their truth, their path, their life. This creates the most beautiful unconditionally loving relationships.

"The secret of change is to focus all your energy on, not on fighting the old, but on building the new." Socrates

It is SO easy to live a life of shoulds and what we were taught how to BE with people. To do what the successful do and then feel unfulfilled. To check to boxes. Live by the 'rules'.

The truth is there is NO rules. Deep inside we KNOW that it (how we are being) is not our path. We have an inner knowing that there is something MUCH bigger and much better. Staying heart centered. Hand over heart and keeping it wide open even when thoughts of fear arise that it may get broken.

In Japan they have a tradition of repairing broken pottery with lacquer mixed with powdered gold. When your heart breaks into a million pieces it is only creating space for MORE love and MORE beauty than you can ever image.

Journal it out!

- Where are you placing judgment on another in your life?

- Where are you taking societal views and projecting them on others?

- Why do you feel right to judge?

- Where do you feel this judgement in your body?

- How can you come from a place of love? Place your hands over your heart and breathe loving breathes into that area. Forgive yourself from coming from a lack of love.

Light Your Soul on Fire

Finding Self Love

Belief: Whatever you say becomes truth – even if it isn't.

Oh yes here it is. Just another story I wrote about myself. I am not worthy. Those word sting just typing them. This is how I felt. I walked down the crumbling stairs into a dark apartment drenched in regret. As I struggled to turn the key my heart skipped a beat. I pushed the heavy door open. Dirty dishes covering the counter, clothes all over the floor, credit card bills piled on the table. Scooter my beloved cat. Most didn't like her, but SHE was authentic. The only thing that made me smile. Was this really my life?

I moved here with a guy that I started dating out of sheer boredom that turned into a nightmare. I felt stuck, living in a dump, in debt, and emotionally drowning. I couldn't do any better. Who would want to be with me? This voice in my head was seriously getting on my nerves. I was about to burst. I threw myself onto the couch crying until my face was covered in hives. Is this REALLY my life? If so, it isn't worth it.

These words I spoke to myself every minute of the day. My self-respect was non-existent. Who is going to love and value me if I don't even value myself? And then it hit me. My intuition LOUD and CLEAR and I decided to step up and listen. Head smack! Duh! First on the agenda of self-love was to take care of me. TO fill me up. To pour into me. To figure out WHO I AM.

I don't know how this moment came about but it was quick, and I was super quick to listen and take massive inspired action. My soul let out WAY louder than a whisper. I went out and got a personal trainer because when you feel good about your body everything else seems to feel easier to heal. And what else would we use those student loans for right?!

Seriously the best personal trainer. He put me into immaculate shape and taught me what my body is really capable of. He gave me the gift of belief when I couldn't see it in myself. There is something about someone else pushing you to be better when you don't see it yourself. He was the start of me having a coach from here on out. Someone to put my blind spots in front of me and show me what I am really made of.

"Surround yourself with the dreamers and the doers, the believers and thinkers, but most of all, surround yourself with those who see the greatness within you, even when you don't see it yourself." Edmund Lee

Like hitting the upper limit and then busting through. That upper limit is something I put there, and I can take it down and move beyond it but only when I believe. I turned around as I was quickly dressing myself for the day. My clothes were feeling amazing but what I saw in the mirror I was not expecting. A lean toned stunning body. Nothing I ever imagined I would look like. It happened quickly, like almost overnight. Transformations happen overnight when you allow yourself to be present and in the moment. Not waiting to see how long it will be when you achieve said desire.... Ponder on that.

I was feeling amazing, taking care of myself and I knew what I need to do next. I called my parents and told them that I was breaking up with my boyfriend of 3 years. I had no idea how I was going to do life by myself, pay my bills, live alone, wallow in my loneliness but anything has got to be better than this! My parents were beyond amazing and stepped up. Whatever they could do to help me to get out they would. My boyfriend was gone, and I packed up everything that was mine. Mom helped me load it up. The conversation was silent as neither of us knew what to say. She could tell I had been crying. The hives seriously gave it away. Why do I always have to get hives when I cry?

As we were driving to my new apartment, I could feel a sense of peace wrapped in a truck load of fear. My intuition screaming at me that this is so right, so I chose to trust it. I really had no choice. It was toxic for me to stay. I got out my car and grabbed the wine glasses, my favorite wine glasses packed tight but quickly in cardboard. My hands shaking. What I am doing touching my favorite wine glasses? I mean for real, I was in no condition to touch ANYTHING fragile. It was like slow motion bouncing back and forth from one hand to the next and then landing right onto the cement with a shatter. I was crushed. Was this a sign? I need to pull it together if I am going to finish unpacking the car. Mom grabbed my hand. She whispers something that calmed everything in me. 'Everything is going to be ok.'

And you know what? It was. It was more than ok! I had my own place. Everything was decorated and organized exactly the way I wanted it. Every single thing in the perfect place, labeled, organized, and peaceful. I realized this was my first experience EVER living alone. My soul was singing, and life was good. A new-found sense of independence. I did not need anyone and financially what I thought wasn't possible was more than possible.

Then it hit me like a ton of bricks. A month or two into living in my new place I was sitting cross legged on the floor trying to retain some corporate banking and economic strategies for my upcoming exam. All I could think about was do I go or not?! The big work party is tonight but I have since been relocated to a different division within the bank.

I have been trying to avoid the social limelight since starting college to keep me laser focused. I don't know if intuition guided me here or not, but it shifted my life forever.

I decided on going and showed up early in the church parking lot just to see the big yellow bus waiting there for us. My old boss and co-workers all incredible people already there and ready to go. We were almost ready to pull out and this guy jumps on that in all seriousness has had my attention for a while. He was the guy in the team meetings that would say the most random jaw dropping things when we all would least expect it. Tonight, was the beginning of a lesson I didn't know I needed to learn. One that created 3 beautiful children and gave me the backbone to TRUELY live an amazing life. One that broke open my heart and allowed me to love deeper and harder.

Re-write

I stand up for me. I choose me above all else. I am worthy of amazing even if there is no evidence yet that it exists. Settling is lack of self-love. I am willing to see it differently. People come into your life for a reason, a season, or a lifetime. Not seeing a solution or the rise of self-doubt is just distrust that the universe isn't powerful enough to carry you when you can't carry yourself. Trust that you are trust fund baby of the universe. Allow yourself to be supported. You can do life on your own OR you can allow in a bigger force – God, Universe, Angels, etc. to do some of your heavy lifting. Trust.

Journal it out!

- Why are you worthy of living an amazing life? This alone will uncover where your belief in unworthiness is hiding.

- Where in your life are you holding yourself back due to a lack of self-love?

- If you loved yourself unconditionally, what would change in your life?

The Parents get a Divorce

I wipe the sleep from my eyes and grab my tea to sit outside in the cool brisk air to take in the beauty of northern Minnesota. I can hear the loons in the distance, and I am at peace, rested, rejuvenated from the energy expended from my wedding the day before. Replaying the day's events of being a princess for a day.

Like clockwork the phone rings and it is my mom on the other end. The sound in her voice like someone just dropped her off a cliff. As the words came out of her mouth piercing my heart and breaking it in a gazillion pieces. Dad and I are getting a divorce. What?!? I can hardly breathe. How could they? How could my family break apart? I just did yesterday what they are undoing. Did I do the right thing. Is marriage even sacred? How could this be happening to me? I was crushed.

My entire family stability shattered, or so I thought. At 27 years old the pain had captivated my entire body. It doesn't matter the age or the circumstances. My honeymoon was beyond ruined, or so I thought. I couldn't cope or though I thought I couldn't. I allowed it to crush the next 6 months of my life and relationships. I would call my Dad and throw all the shrapnel I could at him for wrecking my life. He wanted so bad for me to understand and instead I just wallowed in my self-pity and really my biggest fear. He had triggered it and I was not even close to ready to heal this wound buried deep inside me.

I cried myself to sleep countless nights. I took sides of a war that wasn't even mine. This lesson was a strong and powerful one that took me years to heal from. Society says that the perfect family is one that stays together regardless of how miserable they are right?!

I made the executive decision and decided to cut him out of my life. The guy I idolized and put up on a pedestal. I couldn't bear to think this man wasn't who I thought he was. I forgot he was human.

Months later the phone call rang. It was my sister. 'Dad's getting married'. I had to hold back from throwing up. My worst nightmare just came out of her mouth. How could he? How was I going to accept this? Hasn't he done enough. I made myself the victim. I wrote a story around it. I chose suffering.

The wedding day came, and I waited until the last moment to show up. I could hardly look him in the eye. We took our family pictures and then got a table as far back as I possibly could. The pastor started in. I wanted to plug my ears and pretend I was somewhere else. The tears started to roll down my cheeks. The vows.... My body was screaming please do not do this! Why?!? I lost it. I spend the rest of the ceremony crying my eyes out in the back of the hall. I was feeling selfish. Why is this happening to me? I left as soon as I could, and I took this event and white-ed it out like it didn't even happen. If I lived farther away from home and never came home, I wouldn't have to deal with this.

So, I moved away. I avoided the home I grew up in ALL my childhood. I dove into my immediate growing family and children. I stayed focused on my own life. Abandonment. The repeating pattern that I was still not ready to look at or heal. If you don't feel it. You sure can't heal it. I stuffed it deeper and moved on.

Given a couple years I was able to look back at this lesson and see through my heart that he had chosen him. To honor him. To allow his soul to learn lessons that he needed. That it was never about me or against me. It was a man that decided to stand up. Decided to experience something new. To expand his heart. And with this I now respect and love him for who he is regardless of what he chooses or doesn't choose. My parents both are better because of it. It startled them to wake up. To see their life. To quit living in the vicious cycle of shoulds. My parents' divorce was a blessing to all of us impacted. The healing was profound.

When feelings drop into your awareness of reacting to EVERYTHING, and you notice the emotions that are coming out of you or stuffing feel bad – notice them.

Expectations of ourselves, others, situations, can really send us spiraling the opposite direction in lightning speed. Pulling us out of alignment and into a lack of compassion. Our dark shadow. We all have it. It comes out based upon how we decide to see the world that day.

That's right. It's a decision. Awareness is ALL about seeing how your feel and embracing it. When you stay awake and notice what is going on within you – you can see the deeper shadow. We don't like to believe that we have this – but we ALL do.

Lighten up. Allow the world to do their thing and BE the observer instead of the controller. You were never in control anyway. Control is just fear. Fear that it will not play out exactly the way you EXPECTED. Key word. Expectation.

If you act this way then I will be calm, happy, content, high vibration.

It's a lesson for your soul. Can you see that super flow and surrender is the way to ULTIMATE FREEDOM? Letting go of your idea of how it 'should' go and allowing it to be what it is. Perfection. Divinely guided. Exactly what you need. Can you TRUST it? Can you trust that everything IS working out for you?

There is nothing better (in the evolution of our soul) than life events that break your heart SO hard that it opens up wider that it was able to prior. Allowing us to love more. Love harder. Love deeper.

Re-write

We are all souls inhabiting a human body for a soulful experience. Our hearts get to grow in the learning that love and compassion is the only answer. Self-love is the most beautiful thing we can experience. It is never selfish. I choose to no longer project my ideas on how others should live their lives. I choose to accept ALL exactly the way they are at this very moment. To love un-conditionally but with boundaries. I still get to get treated with love or you are not allowed in my life. Fair enough?

Be gentle in this journaling. Chances are there are a lot of triggers here. Relationships are some of our biggest teaching in this school of life. Let that be ok. Allow yourself to find the lesson and the growth. Allow yourself to set your soul free from the bondage of projection. You deserve happiness.

Journal it out!

- Where are you allowing your head and other's beliefs to affect your thoughts about yourself and others?

- Where can you open your heart further and allow it to stay open?

- Where can you sprinkle in more unconditional love to others and respect their journeys?

- What stories are negatively impacting the relationships in your life? How

  can you shift them and see them differently?

Going Against the Grain

Many of my friends were frustrated taking pregnancy test after pregnancy test with negative results. I wanted to be prepared that it could be part of my journey and I didn't want to be in my 30s still having kids. So, after the wedding we started 'trying'. I woke up rolled out of bed or maybe fell out of bed and was oh so sick. I stumbled to the bathroom catching my foot on the door and hit the floor. Sitting on the cold floor head pressed against my bathtub to keep cool I knew it. I was pregnant. I was every form of wasn't ready. How did this happen so fast? As the nausea subsided, I started to feel the excitement and in the back of my throat of what did I just do. It is probably a blessing that nobody tells you what this whole parenting thing is about.

My back aches, my head is pounding and all I want to do is lay on the floor and moan. I was such a baby. I barely survived pregnancy and I only had a couple weeks to go. I had had a personal trainer and my diet was decent, but I let it all go during pregnancy. The story I told was I can eat all I want when I am pregnant. Once for me and once for baby.

The hormones took over my body like an alien living there. I could barely move. If I didn't put my shoes on in the morning, they wouldn't go on and if I took them off, they were not going back on. Imagine a pregnant blimp and that is what I looked like and felt like. Time was flying by and I needed to get my ducks in a row. I was nowhere ready to be a mom and lord knows I needed all the help I could get. I started researching baby products to figure out what I was going to buy for our new little guy. Oh, was I in for a treat? I looked at the top brands for babies and did you know the toxicity levels in them are unbelievable.

I went on a super pregnant hormonal mission to find a solution for this new child coming into the world as I was not about to settle. I was invited to a class to learn about holistic ways to treat common ailments without putting harmful chemicals on myself and my kids. At first, I am not going to lie. I thought it was a cult. Lavender can do what? Frankincense to stop a cough? What?! Get out of town. But my mom, bless her heart said we were jumping in with both feet. This was the start of my holistic journey. I started down the road less traveled and I became a closet user of essential oils and other holistic remedies. My entire life I worked so hard just to fit in that this was well out of my comfort zone. It wasn't about me anymore and my child and future children deserve vibrant health.

I turned into a closet oiler. When I started essential oils were not a thing. So, I snuck them around the best I could so nobody would see when we were in public. Prior to having kids, I had a handful of holistic friends and I always wondered why and what their problem was. Judgmental and not willing to learn about it. Everyone is going to get cancer anyway so what was the point right?! I had my blinders up and it was my job to keep this little guy healthy and happy. Talk about massive life shift. This was the first of many to come. Remember now this decision was made from a place of fear.

The next two kids followed close behind. They came fast and furious and it put me right in the trenches not ever knowing if I was coming or going. Looking back this was a choice. I didn't prioritize self-care. I didn't pay attention to myself. I just did my 'should' give everything I have and hope it all works out.

This oil thing turned out to be a blessing in disguise. It was that nasty pyramid scheme thing you know your uncle told you never to get into. Well I was knee deep in it and I wasn't able to hide it anymore. The business took off and I decided to get on the ride to see where it would go. You see all things important to me were freedom, time and financial, health, and emotional balance. This gave me ALL of this as well as an income stream as I was headed into the divorce.

Truth is don't judge a book by its cover. Grow a set. Yell at the top of the mountain all about a solution you find that WORKS! Don't be a sissy like me. Nature has crazy amazing healing power. Do what feels good and aligned for you. For real.

Re-Write

Pregnancy is not that hard. Trust your body. Listen to it. Release ALL the stories about other's experiences. You manifest the story you tell. Want it to be hard? Then preach that story to the world!

Or how about nothing is really hard nor good nor bad. It is just IS. No judgement. We make things 'mean something' and like to define it. The belief systems that back struggle tend to be ones of no pain – no gain, or struggle gets results. How crazy does that sound?! What if instead our belief was align to what feels good and take inspired action and know that you will get what you desire OR something better. It really can be easy. Easy not lazy. Easy is never lazy. Lazy is neither good or bad. It just is.

Journal it out!

- What are you deciding is hard?

- What decisions are you making out of fear?

- Where in your life do you KNOW you can incorporate healthier options?

- Where can you omit turning a blind eye for the sake of you and your family?

- How can it get better than this?

Light Your Soul on Fire

Losing it Before I Knew it

My youngest was 9 months old, I was nursing, how could I be pregnant again? Seriously what is in the water I am drinking?! I couldn't believe that the test was positive. You are not supposed to get pregnant when you are nursing right?! Once the acceptance set in the joke was 'it is going to be twins'. I mean seriously I could barely handle the two I already had. How was I going to throw a third one into the mix? (A little insider information: I prayed hard for 4 children for a long time.) My plan was always to have two close and wait a couple years and have two more back to back. Was I upset that I was pregnant or was I upset that was not in alignment with my plan?

I was angry. Like beyond enraged. Why would this happen? If I had to be totally honest with you. I wanted out of this marriage. I was borderline miserable, and I KEPT getting pregnant. Like I didn't know how it happens. I promised myself I wouldn't make any crazy decisions like ending a marriage when I was SUPER hormonal and/or pregnant.

Side note: And possibly off topic... but did you women know that when you are emotional and a bit crazy during your time of the month, the time where your body releases what it doesn't need. Yes, that time! You are releasing emotions that you have suppressed otherwise during the month. It is a grand time for introspection of what feelings are REALLY coming up? Look at them. Feel them. Quit suppressing them so that the crazy lady doesn't have to come out every month. It is a gift to know what is really going on. FEEL it all. Heal it. Communicate it. Release it. You are worth it.

Ok back to the story. This is hard to tell. Who gets angry when they get pregnant? One that doesn't trust the bigger plan. The plan that was never mine? The woman that just needs to surrender her stories and ways of life that she thinks is best. I was SO angry. SO mad. For the first THREE months I rejected this pregnancy. I wish I would have talked to someone. The lesson for me here was RADICAL ACCEPTANCE. One that this control freak really knew nothing about. (P.S. Control is just fear.)

The birth of my second child was traumatic, and the hospital was very brash at allowing me to have a say in how I wanted my delivery to go.

The decision was then made for #3 to have a home water birth. Yay crazy right!? I was nervous but excited that I could do this the way I wanted on my terms AND honor my body and my baby. Control issues? The pregnancy was amazing. Maybe it takes 3 pregnancies to understand your body and what you need. Either way I was grateful.

The days were approaching, and I had all my supplies ready that my midwife asked me to get. We had very little medical intervention throughout the pregnancy beside the visits with our midwife. We got the 20-week basic ultrasound just to make sure everything was kosher, and the results assured me that we were right on track. The jokes were still strong from many friends in my circle that this must be twins. That would be my luck.

Don't you know 1:00 am in the morning my contractions start strong and steady, I can barely breathe. Don't tell me she is going to fall out as fast as the others. My midwife has an hour drive as does my mom. Nobody is here to watch the kids. Am I ready for this? Should we just go the hospital. The pain is almost unbearable. What was less than an hour felt like an eternity. Everyone was arriving and setting up and I was trying to make it through to get into the tub.

Finally, I was in. The water took me too another world. The pain intensity started to diminish. I started to surrender to the contractions instead of fighting it. I could feel her starting to come out. Not even one push and she was safely on my chest with a blanket keeping her warm partially submerged in the water.

Her eyes. Piercing to my soul. Her energy was that of a comfort I have never felt. Then the placenta came out and now I have seen the last two and this looked different. I didn't give any more attention to it. Back to the beautiful baby. The one I so resented at the beginning of the pregnancy. Which I know completely regretted AND felt horrible about.

We got out of the tub and into the bed all cleaned up. I was in awe of the smooth process still remembering the intense pain. One hour and 15 minutes from start to finish. That felt like a record. The connection was strong from the start. We just gazed into each other's eyes in complete and utter joy.

I could hear whispering from the bathroom. The midwives were cleaning up. When they walked into the bedroom their faces were long. Maybe they were tired?

'You had another baby that didn't make it.' She looked to have made it to 18 weeks old. I was carrying twins. I lost a baby. My heart sunk. To a place I didn't even know existed. Did I do this? Did the anger and resentment I had towards all this create the loss of a child? Or was God helping out and knowing that I could have never handled 4? The questions kept coming. The answers still have never surfaced.

I am supposed to be happy right now and all I want to do is scream on the top of my lungs. What did I do wrong? Why me?

The next six months were quite interesting as I was living a life part sad and part happy. Crying and laughing every day. But not allowing myself to heal anything. Grief can be funny. The story I told was one of IF I heal it then I am saying it is ok and I accept it. It took 4 years to really allow myself to feel it. To forgive myself for being angry. For forgiving myself for doing the best I could with what I knew at the time. For loving myself hard. For all the regret. For the missing pieces in my heart that I don't know will ever be repaired and whole again.

Re-write

Loss can be a blessing. I can empathize and FEEL how others that also experience this go though. Pain that breaks the heart open allows me to love more and deeper at a level that wasn't available before. We are just souls in a human body and death is just energy shifting into a higher vibration.

We can still connect with those on the other side if we allow ourselves to. They speak to us with signs, synchronicities, through mediums, or directly through us. We are spiritual beings in a human body. Here to experience and grow our souls.

This a playground and a play of sorts. I allow my soul to grow. I allow to see the blessings and heal the pain. I choose to feel it all. To see this life differently than I did prior. I choose to live life with my heart wide open. Full of love and compassion.

Journal it out!

- Where in your life have you experienced loss that you have yet to heal?

- What is preventing you from healing? The 20 minutes of excruciating pain

  that can give you a lifetime of freedom.

- What story are you telling that is preventing you from releasing the pain?

- How can you see this differently?

Following Societies Path

Cup of my favorite tea in hand sitting on my kitchen floor, the tears started to fall one by one hitting the worn-out wooden floor. From the outside my life looked nothing short of perfect. 10 years ago, I made the life checklist that I allow society ingrained into my being. Get a 4-year degree. Check. Get an amazing job with lots of opportunity. Check. Find a tall dark and handsome man to marry. Check. Get married. Check. Buy the perfect house. Check. Have 2.5 children. Check.

I did EVERYTHING I was supposed to do. Why do I feel so empty inside? Why is this hole in me so big? Why can't I just be grateful to have the picket fence life? What more could I possible have to fill this miserable hole? I had this amazing life plan to grow old with the father of my children holding hands on the porch of a beautiful home overlooking the water.

A veil I couldn't see through. I built my life around a set of checklists. Someone else's truths. My passion for life was NON-existent. The checklist was one that would accomplish a life of happily ever after. I naturally love setting goals, so this was fun for me. Or was it? Was I running from something instead? Until I hit the dead end. I followed the yellow brick road. What I didn't do was follow my authenticity. I never asked Becca what she wanted, how she felt, where she wanted to go, what excited her. A life based on fear of doing everything right. What was I so afraid of?

Why did I believe that the 'desired' path is for everyone? Where did I learn this?

To be born the person we are at the time we were born is 1 in 400 TRILLION! That is crazy talk! That means NO two of us are alike. AT ALL! So why would a single path be good for multiples of people? It doesn't exist. We each have our own beautiful path and we tap into this via intuition, and our inner guidance. We all have 'the feeling' we have just been taught not to use it. To do the should instead of what our body is telling us. To follow societies truths even when it doesn't feel good. To hustle and drive and burn out because THEN you are worthy.

Busy as a badge of honor. When in honesty and truth we are human BEINGS. We are meant to be not do. I chose to burn it ALL down and start over. Find myself and choose me and my guidance from here on out. And damn does it feel good.

Loving message to YOU:

What are you waiting for?!

Decide that you are no longer available for the crap story you are telling. Seriously! Be done!

You get to have it ALL!

You get to FEEL the way you want to feel!

You are ALWAYS supported!

Trust! Then leap!

Re-write

My life is my design. I manifest it all based on my thoughts and beliefs. I will let this be easy and trust my inner guidance always.

Journal it out!

- What doesn't feel like an exhale in your life?

- Where do you need to create space and release old thoughts, beliefs, habits?

- How can you shift TODAY so you don't crash tomorrow?

Putting the Bags Down

An amazing mentor walked into my life and called me out. She saw me picking up others baggage and claiming it as my own. I was poisoning myself and I didn't even know it. I felt heavy as if I was trudging through life with a zoo full of monkeys on my back. I had no idea that I was doing this to myself.

I was so excited to be on my way with my oldest to meet with some amazing business partners and mentors. We crossed the street and dodged the cars and we made our way into this restaurant. It reminded me of the old men's club. I expected old wise men smoking cigars which you can't do in Minnesota anymore. As we heaved the door open my son stayed super close to me. It was packed. The energy was heightened with laughing, uplifting conversation, and what looked like yummy food. We made our way through the back bumping into a couple people accidently. We were the foreigners as everyone looked at us knowing we were not locals.

We made it to the restaurant area, and it felt comforting and spacious. Perfect for Brady to relax and be a kid and for me to connect with some amazing women. Mysterious and distant a woman walks in and sits at our table. Confident, established, and intriguing. She instantly takes over the conversation. I can't help but draw into her as she speaks just observing her every move. There is something different about her. I couldn't put my finger on it.

We all got to know each other better and dished out probably every quarter out of my purse for the arcade. Little did I know this new friend would become a pivotal mentor on my journey.

You could say that she gave me the tools to start facing my fears and dealing with the 'what is' in a healthier way. Oh, the what is. It is hard to confront the very thing you have been avoiding for years or maybe a lifetime. Do you ever feel yourself saying but 'if I just did this then it would get better?'

I poured myself into being successful, defined by everyone but me. This amazing mentor helped me to look at my shadows and my choices in a different light. The light was and still is bright and sometimes blinding. Painful and emotional. I committed to myself that I will find my path and my purpose, and I vowed to trust in the process. God, Universe, or whatever you would like to call it now became a stronger influence and strength in my life. I asked it in. I allowed and trusted even when it didn't make logical sense. I made choices based on intuition instead of logic.

The only thing going through my head as I stepped through the threshold and pushed my fears aside was... God I can't wait to see how you pull this off. Deer in the headlights. Yes. I wasn't going to attempt this alone.

Re-write

Life is only how you perceive it. Change your perception as well as understanding and well... change your life. A shadow is only an aspect of our self that we haven't looked at and healed. It would be like ignoring the dirt pile in the corner. Knowing it is dirty. Semi-annoyed with the dirt. But choosing not to see it.

Think of the 20 seconds it will take to LOOK at the dirt and then sweep it out. Moving on. It is that easy.

Tony taught me that our choices are made by the perceived joy or pain we get from deciding. We can lose the weight, but is the process joyful or painful? How we define this will tell us how the result ends. If we define it as painful – we will never lose the weight. At least not permanently. In the process we will lower our vibration which directly impacts the rest of our life. Only attracting into our lives that level of vibration – which isn't what we desire.

Re-write the process as it being joyful. Visualize the joy. Then watch the results come as if by magic.

Journal it out!

- What are you no longer available for?

- What corners need to be swept? What cobwebs need to be cleaned up?

- What story are you telling about the process? Hard or easy? Joyful or painful?

- How can you re-write your story to get the desired results? A life of joy and happiness?

- Why are you not worthy of having this joyful life? (Write here until you can't come up with anything else. THEN burn it.) This process releases the unworthiness out of you. Feel the lightness in your body from doing this. Do this as many times as you need to – to get out of your own way.

Light Your Soul on Fire

Doing it for ME

Sitting in my comfy chair at my desk doing the daily grind at my amazing corporate job and the phone rings. I answer...my jaw drops. The New York accent is strong and the male
voice bolsters away with questions on my products that are coming faster than I can answer. After losing my breath trying to keep up the voice on the other end of the phone stops. 'Can we schedule a meeting at my office?' I take a deep breath and glance at my schedule. I will be in your area next Wednesday and have an opening at 11 and it was our only opening left. Perfect and it was scheduled. And the call ended. I just sat there staring at my screen like I got hit by a verbal bus. I walked back to my tiny apartment that evening lost in a confusion of energy.

The next week my partner and I show up at the office and present our products just as we have been doing all week for other clients. This meeting was different. I should have expected it. The energy in the room was vibrating the walls. It felt incredible. The questions continued to come as a quicker pace. Who is this guy? Where did he come from?

We agreed to lunch. I jumped into the back of his Mercedes and my partner in the front. We stopped at this quaint little restaurant in the midst of the hustle and bustle of this beautiful tropical city. We were seated, and the magic began.

The conversation flowed. Did I know him? I was so confused. It was like we have known each other all our lives, sharing food, conversations with an energy that usually comes from the excitement of a best friend. We left, and my partner asked me what just happened. I had no idea. This guy intrigued me.

As we worked together more mostly via phone, we got to know each other. My job was building relationships and I was really good at it. I started to wonder if this guy was stalking me as it almost looked like we were twins living in different states. We have the same birthday, favorite foods, favorite color, personality traits, family backgrounds, goals, aspirations, although he was well ahead of me in the process. It started to feel like I was talking to myself.

This relationship started to bring a rollercoaster of emotions. Our strong traits clashed, and I approached our friendship with choices based on fear. What if he wasn't who he said he was. What if he really was stalkerish? I mean who has these many things in common, thinks the same way, and literally has the same personality. What is going on here? The friendship grew quickly, and it started to feel like I had met my identical twin. The entire experience completely bizarre but perfect.

I was driving home one night from a late night 5k run in the midst of the city with some fabulous friends. I could barely keep my eyes open, so I dialed his number. He picked up. We talked about the night. Light conversation and then it hit me. This was going to be the last time we spoke. He didn't know it or maybe he did. Two days later I was married. I vowed to push out all of my male friends as I didn't want to make my new husband uneasy in any way. I thought it was the right thing to do.

Have you ever had a connection like this? A soul connection?

He was there to talk to about anything which became one of the oddest but most profound relationships of my life. He knew things about me that I wish I would have listened to. Looking back, he was there to help me find my authentic self. I was so scared. The FEAR was heavy. I heard him, but I never took his advice. Frustrating for him for sure. He saw things I didn't. He saw me walking into a completely un-aligned life. He told me. I listened. I chose fear instead. Then I pushed him out.

For years we never spoke, and I got the nudge to reach out. To catch up. It felt like we never missed a beat. Little did I know at the time – it was the start of the end of my marriage. I knew then but didn't know. If that makes any type of sense. His beginning advice became profound as life went on. Maybe it was for the journey I was navigating, and he knew it? We will never know.

When people come into your life. Trust that they are supposed to be there. For a reason, a season, or a lifetime. It was a serendipitous for sure. Trust your intuition. Take a risk. You can't mess this life this up. Because we are here to learn.

Re-write

We are given the gift of intuition. I could have potentially avoided the mis-alignment if I were to just trust. Trust that others have the best intentions. That fear is made up. That life is a culmination of experiences that will literally give you the ride of your life. There is no such thing as black and white. Ride the waves. Feel the breeze. Life is short. When others relay messages to you – hear them. Feel them. Then check in. What feels right to you? Not safe. But right.

Journal it out!

- Where in your life is mis-aligned? What is feeling kinked?

- Who in your life is waiting to help guide you?

- What fears have you created that are preventing you from moving forward?

- How are you not being present to see the gift of beautiful souls waiting to bless your life right in front of you?

Light Your Soul on Fire

Getting Fired

I slipped my flip flops on under my large pregnant belly. The air was chilled as I stepped outside. A neighbor drove by and waved. Is summer here yet. I was so ready to wear my flip flops without freezing my toes. I opened the mailbox. A letter from the courthouse? I feverishly opened it up wondering what this could be. Jury duty. Well that is convenient. My heart sank. I wonder how I am going to get out of this one. I was 8 months pregnant. I have a ton of work to catch up on before leave.

The timing couldn't have been worse, or was it a blessing? I went into work the next morning to chat with my boss. I was already pushing for a 4-month maternity leave. Although this was out of my control, I was dreading what they would say. I didn't know anyone that got called in, so I brushed it off hoping that it wouldn't be me. I called in on Sunday night and lo and behold I HAD to go in.

I walked into the courthouse that next Monday, the musty air making me feel uncomfortable. My whole-body squirming like I did something wrong. Jury duty was a new experience. I waddled in because seriously this baby was getting ready to fall out and everyone was staring at me.

I didn't want to draw attention. I went through security and turn the corner into the check in area and then into a room stuffed full of very unhappy people. Nobody wanted to be there. How could I sit in this toxic energy all morning? We were stuffed like sardines. I was hot, and my butt was going numb sitting and waiting.

We sat in this room ALL day with no word on what was next. A beautiful blonde walked in frazzled and hurried. The news was not accepted by the crowd. We were to all return tomorrow to start the interview process. 8:00 am the next days I was plopped back in the same seat now feeling content that I have a great book to immerse myself into while I practice patience. By 3:00 I was finally called. They take me into the courtroom, and I waddle into the stand. The front row is filled with 4 plus lawyers and the defendant. I feel like I am going to throw up. The guilt in the back of my throat. Why am I here!? What is this! They ask me questions in a yes or no format. My heart sinks, it's a first-degree murder case. I am already a hormonal mess, they will for surely not pick me. My hands are shaking uncontrollably, and my contractions start up. I start to sweat and then the questions stop.

I am dismissed. I wasn't prepared for this. Can I go now. Nope. They escort me back to the stuffy room to sit in for the remainder of the day. Back to my book. The blonde hustles into dismiss us. My body slumps, back again tomorrow morning. This goes on for the ENTIRE week.

Friday arrives where we find out who has been chosen to be on the jury panel. I grip my old faded red chair positioning myself and praying that it isn't me. Why can't I get out of this?

I have just missed an entire week of work and my employer is not happy! I am so behind. The feeling of defeat comes over me as she calls my name. I can't watch violent shows on tv without having nightmares. How am I going to do this 8 months pregnant?!

We are dismissed. I go home covered in tears. I am to be back on Monday as the trial starts. I spend the next two weeks with this beautiful baby pressing on my bladder, hungry all the time, and contractions on and off hoping to not go into labor as the prosecution goes through all the evidence. It was horrible and hard to sit through. Was this really happening?

What kind of humans would do something like this? I can barely hold myself together being in the same room as someone that could have done these selfish acts.

The prosecution rests and I have all of this on my heart with no-one to talk to. My shoulders feel heavy, my feet hurt, and we are back to our tiny jury room. We get a break and I get to relieve my poor bladder. How is this child going to turn out with the stress I have put on her going through this process?

They call us back into the courtroom. They announce that we will be sequestered. Say what? They are taking us from our families, with no access to communication, and no idea on when we will be back. I have nobody to watch my kiddo and I have 2 hours to go home and pack and make any arrangements. I run to my car.

Who is going to watch my little guy? The tears are pouring out. I slam my door shut. Why me?! My sobs are intense it is hard to breathe. I frantically call my mom at work and she can't make out a word I say. As she calms me down, she agrees to come straight to my house and will watch my little guy until I get out. I pick him up at daycare, my face is covered in hives and I still can't control the crying. I assure my amazing daycare provider that I am ok.

Deep inside I am not. My kids' father is 7 states away on work. The pressure and stress this have caused has pushed me past my breaking point. My anger sets in. Why me... why me!?

My mom shows up and I am packed and ready to go. I drive back to the courthouse and we park in a non-descript area. They usher us into a private room in the back of the courthouse. My contractions are getting stronger as I sit down in a board room. The evidence is brought in and put in the middle of the table. They walk us through what is required of us to come to a verdict. We are not allowed to leave until we do. After over indulging in pizza to soothe my wide range of hormonal emotions we are escorted to a hotel to a room with a guard standing outside. There is no tv, or radio or anything to do.

We are required to give up our cell phones, purses etc. when we got there, and someone had already gone through my luggage to make sure we have nothing. I lay on the bed exhausted and frustrated staring at the ceiling paying close attention to the water spots. I can't sleep. The case running through my head and the nightmare I have had to listen to in the previous weeks. I feel so alone. The seclusion is making me crazy and the contractions are getting stronger.
What if I go into labor? I drift off to nightmare land.

I wake from an obnoxious guard outside my door. I quickly shower and hustle into our transportation back into the courthouse. Back to our stuffy room that still had the smell of pizza lingering. I am starving. Doughnuts and orange juice for breakfast. Come on. My body can't handle the heavy load of sugar.

My body can't handle any of this. My son is at the forefront of my mind. Is he ok? Does he know his mama is coming back? Does he feel abandoned?

Day 2 begins. We go through more of the evidence. I don't want to touch it. This whole case makes me sick to my stomach. The end of the day is closing and still we are deadlocked. 7 not guilty and 3 guilty. Back to the hotel. Will this nightmare ever end? Another night of staring at the ceiling. I am running out of things to count.

I pass out fully clothed. My body turned to jelly.

The next morning, we are back at it. You can feel the tension rise in the room. I keep my breathing slow and steady to keep my contractions from getting too painful. By lunch as we have come to a decision. We now wait while the lawyers and defendant are called back to the courtroom. We sit around eating more pizza. You can see the fatigue in everyone's faces. We have become friends through this process. We have little to talk about and little energy to want to talk. The windows are covered so we can't even look outside. Boxed into a jail cell. Are we done yet?

Finally, hours later we file into our seats, me almost tripping. The defendant staring at each of us. I try not to make eye contact. You can see the energy in the room is almost non-existent. The head of our jury is instructed to bring our final decision to the Judge. My heart sinks. The Judge reads the form we all signed off on. Guilty. We are each individually asked in front of a packed courtroom if we agree to the verdict. My voice shaky but firm answers with a yes. Hopeful that our verdict was to the best of our ability altering someone else life for the rest of their existence. Guilty of first-degree murder. It's over.

I speed home to my son, and I hold him and cry so grateful to be in his presence again. So grateful the nightmare has ended. The next day – Friday I did not contact my work. I was in a rough mental state and needed a day to pull myself back together.

Monday morning, I woke feeling refreshed and energized as a mom ready to give birth in the weeks to come. I walk into work ready to clean out the pile that has built up while I have been locked in at the courthouse.

My supervisor meets me at my office and asks me to come see her. She shuts the door. My lip starts to quiver, and my hands feel a little shaky. Something seems off. 'We feel that you are not a good fit, you are fired.' My heart sinks into my gut. Who is going to hire me? Where am I going to work? WHAT am I going to do? I hold back tears. What are others going to think? Fired?!

I have failed. She gives me a box of my personal possessions and walks me out. Shock runs through my body. What am I going to do? My world is crumbling around me. I cry the entire way home. Fired. Fired. Who is going to hire a pregnant lady ready to give birth any day?

As the days pass, I found the gratitude for allowing myself to spend the next week one on one with my son loving up on him and experiences life through his eyes. I wake up in the middle of the night. My water broke.... did it? Am I peeing myself? Seriously these hormones. Gah, I am a mess. Labor is in full gear. I slide down the stairs slowly on my butt as the contractions are getting stronger and closer. I get to the middle of the yard and need to sit. I can't even stand through the contractions. I am praying and praying for help. God I can't do this without you. The neighbor isn't home.

I can't make it much longer. We take our son with us to the hospital. I sit in the back seat with him. He holds me. I feel every bump and the pain is almost unbearable. 10 miles felt like 100. I get positioned in the wheelchair. The pressure is intense. She wants out and I am not ready. My son sits on my lap and holds me tight. He eases my pain with his touch and kisses. Our lives soon to be forever changed. They check me, and I am ready now. No time for
pain relief.

The room goes white. I am in another world. I can barely see the people in the room. The sounds suddenly disappear. Where am I? I push. I can't do this. Words come out of my mouth I can never take back.

She is out. The white haze disappears, and a beautiful loud crying baby is on my chest. A sigh of relief comes over my entire body.

A beautiful little princess. She is perfect. Days later we go home. Financial pressure #nojob is on, but my lack of sleep inhibits me from being able to think logically. I pour myself into these beautiful babes. I surround myself in gratitude.

Re-write

We all have moments in our life where we have decided that we have failed. We fail to see the blessings that come from changes in our life – ones we couldn't have predicted. But then again. Life is not predictable. So, it is funny when we believe that it should be. Surrender was a big lesson in this life event. The stories I made this event mean. The victim mentality I picked up in the process.

Failure is always perceived. Looking back this was one of the best things that happened to me. The growth and tenacity that I built over this situation gave me the staying ability for what was to come.

This or something better. It is usually always something better.

Journal it out!

- What events in your life are you still holding onto the perceived

    failure?

- What are you making it mean?

- How can you re-write it to showcase the blessings that came out of it?

- How can you allow yourself to see this in a different light?

- Who do you need to forgive?

- How would it feel to hold the belief that everyone is doing the best they can with what they know?

The Walls Come Crashing In

My husband at the time is traveling like crazy for work. I am just getting the hang of loving up on my two beautiful littles and settling into my newly created stay at home mom roll. Our little girl is almost 3 months old. Daddy is supposed to come home today. We clean up the house. My neighbor comes over to help watch the kids, so I can squeeze in a shower. Ah the luxuries.

We wait patiently in the garage and playing in the yard waiting for their daddy to arrive. He parks and walks up. The energy is off. I can feel it. He doesn't make eye contact. He picks up Brady with overflowing love. He looks me in the eye. He says we need to talk. I can't even get a word in when it comes blurting out with a smirk... 'I want a divorce'. Everything freezes. What is going on? I am still in a daze from lack of sleep. Did I just hear you right?

You want what? Why? He refused to talk about it. I bring the kids into the house quickly making sure the neighbors don't see me as I start to fall apart.

I have no job, no form of income, and a new baby. I fall into the couch. He agrees to talk about it. He opens up. 'I can't do this anymore. I am not happy. I want a divorce.'

I am floored. Not a word has been said of this and we enter the eggshell walk. I beg him to change his mind. Is there someone else? I promise to do anything to make it better. My hormones are out of control and my emotions follow. I spent the next 3 days in tears. The feeling of abandonment is eminent.

The walls come crashing. I promised that I would never divorce. I don't believe in it. I am a fighter. I will not walk away. My sister steps in to watch my kids. I am worthless in the parental realm. I cannot function in a world of fog. The more friends I talk to the worse it gets.

I have victimized myself. I took away my ability to stand on my own two feet. Weeks later he boxes his stuff up and moves out. I didn't think it would happen. I had a false sense of hope.
What is wrong with me? What did I do? Where is my strength. What am I going to do?

I was so set on the belief that I needed someone in my life. I wasn't interested in seeing anything else but this working. Even if it was miserable. I mean that is what my parents did for years. Isn't that what marriage is? Just tough it out?

Days later I get a phone call. He wants to come back. Not because he wants to be with me but because he can't live with being away from his children. The rebuilding process begins.

Re-write

So many red flags here that I refused to see. The neat thing about life is that you can't really mess this up. The lessons for your soul will come even if you decide to resist them for a while. I can put a paper bag over my head, so I can't see what is going on, but it will continue to resurface – until I learn the lesson.

Remember our souls came here at this time to learn things we can't learn on the other side. To grow and experience earth and all the things in a human body. We had a clear set of soul growth goals we desired to accomplish while we are here. Other souls agreed to work with us and play certain parts. But we come here. We are born – and we forget ALL of this.

Mine specifically are mastering relationships. Yippee huh. For my entire life. I think I am doing well so far. All my 'issues' have shown up within relationships. But the growth is PROFOUND. More on this later. Xo

Journal it out!

- What lessons are repeating continually in your life?

- Same people or different people?

- Would you be open to learning the lesson now instead of ending

  the relationship and learning it with someone or something else?

- What does your soul want you to know now? Journal this out as a stream of consciousness in letting whatever comes out of your pen without judgement. It is one of my favorite ways to journal.

Love letter to YOU:

Relationships are what make the world go round.

We crave them.

Can't live without them.

They are also our biggest teachers.

They highlight our shadows. The lower vibrational aspects of ourselves. They bring out the ugly at times.

Only showing us what needs to be healed within us.

When we love and approve of ourselves exactly the way we are in this very moment …. our relationships improve!

Improve your relationship with YOU and watch the world shift around you.

You are worthy of having it all. You are perfect exactly the way that you are!

xo

Becca

Light Your Soul on Fire

The Start of the End

Standing at the kitchen island taking in the heavy aroma of the cheese dip and cleaning up the amazing food made for our going away party - wondering why my then husband left early to go to the coffee shop while all our friends are still here. I mean they were here to say goodbye to us. Not a word was spoken most of the weekend between us. It was Sunday night and I was left wondering what it was that I did again. Why the silence?

I like to think that I am direct and respectful and if something is going on, I will be the first to speak up about it. Friday night (the night before) was girl's night at the neighbors and I was so excited to go. It would be the last time that I could walk over and hang out with an amazing inspiring group of gals.

He showed up late super happy not even acknowledging that I was going to be 2 hours late. I felt disrespected. I left and enjoyed the time I had. When I returned home to find him sleeping on the couch. Abnormal but not surprising. I mean it's not like we had the perfect marriage.

Sunday morning when I woke, I found him sleeping in the kids' room. What was he avoiding?

My answer came Sunday night. He walked into the door from the coffee shop and slammed his worn leather shoulder bag of books onto the freshly cleaned granite countertop and the words that came out of his mouth stung deep into my core. I knew before he even opened his mouth. 'I didn't cheat on you.' I took a deep breath and almost allowed my eyes to close. I felt a sigh of relief. I knew this was the beginning of the end.

Deep within my intuition I knew where this was headed. He met a girl a work and became really close with her. She had told her husband Friday night that she was in love with him.

Was this the push we needed. Was she the blessing that allowed this toxic life to unravel? All the pieces started making sense. He was avoiding me trying to wrap his head around what he was going to say. As I laid my head on my pillow later that evening, I started to allow all the feelings that were coming to the surface be acknowledged.

I needed to find myself in a place of acceptance sooner than later. I promised myself everything was going to be ok. Or so I thought.

Re-write

We choose our feelings. We get to decide how this really goes. We can respond, or we can react. We can take a deep breath and walk away – still honoring everything we are feeling. We must FEEL it to heal it. The 20 minutes of pain. Finding where we feel it IN our body, focusing on it to feel it completely and then allowing it to release. Like a stranger passing by on the busy streets of Manhattan. So, it doesn't settle into our cells and negatively impact us the rest of our life.

Emotional discord that hasn't been resolved manifest itself in the body as dis-ease. Longstanding resentment festers itself into cancer. Louise Hay does a great job explaining this in detail in her book – How to Heal Your Life.

Surrender. Surrender... I really mean this. Let go of your stories. Your expectations. Your ideas of the HOW. Trust with every piece of you that everything is happing for YOU. Not to you. That there is a rainbow that always comes after the rain. How long do you want to sit out in the rain? You get to decide. Stand up. You are worth it.

"When you let go, you create space for something better." Unknown

Attachment to anything...

a story

a human

a belief that no longer benefits you

a way of life

stuff

...creates suffering.

When you can allow yourself to surrender it all and be joyful in this very moment – allowing the universe to create magic in your life.

You have found heaven on earth.

Surrender it all.

Journal it out!

- What discord are you manifesting in your body?

- How can you approach life changes going forward in a healthier way?

- What do you need to surrender now to create more joy in your life?

- What is going on right now that you could shift to allow the blessings to unfold?

- Where do you desire to trust more in your life?

- How can you allow your life to be amazing RIGHT NOW?!

Light Your Soul on Fire

The Healing House

The paperwork was signed. The house would be going up for sale in a couple days. If we could just break even, I would be thrilled! I turned a couple different lights on, diffused some essential oils, made sure the throw pillows were in the perfect place to cover up the markings on the couch. I loaded up all the kids in the car and came back in. Where are we going to live once this sells? Is it going to sell? I dropped to my knees and kissed the floor. God will you please help us to sell this fast? I blessed the house and drove off with the kids. Lo and behold 3 days later we had 3 incredible offers and sold our house for well over what we asked. Prayers were answered. With great ease. I was totally in surrender. Manifesting success!

Now onto organizing the boxing of items, donating what no longer serves us, oh yes and where to live next? I spent weeks searching different rental websites. I was so excited to rent. So excited to no longer think about house renovations or fixing anything for that matter. This house was more than overwhelming for me and I was pumped to lift that off my shoulders.

I drug the kids all around the cities trying to find the perfect fit. From townhome to townhome to missed naps to dreaded townhome. Oh yes, they were asking if we could just live in our old home. I felt the same way. So, I set my intentions. I wanted this place to feel spacious, relaxed, and upgrade to where we lived, and I wanted the kids to love it! Not much to ask right?

If you are new to manifesting – your thoughts become things. If you act and believe like you don't already have it – you won't. If you are attached to a specific outcome – chances are you will push it away. If you can feel it, taste it, as if it is already yours – manifesting magic! We all manifest using the universal laws – we just don't realize sometimes that it works if you use it well. It is like gravity. It's a law of the universe. Do you question it? Check to see if it still applies? Probably not.

The law of attraction. Your thoughts/feelings become things. You can get to a point where you manifest what you WANT with ease.

I will show you how.

Create your desire. How you want it to feel and any specifics that are deal breakers. Lean into this feeling. Feel it in your heart all the way to your fingertips.

A spacious, relaxed home. Upgrade from the last home. Kids love it. Safe neighborhood for my family. Great space to be able to start over. To move into the next stages of single parenting and such. A place to heal my heart and release and grow.

Now surrender it up to the universe. I asked God to guide me to the perfect place. And guided I was. The most beautiful home. Filled with chandeliers. Overlooking a large pond with a beautiful trail around it. Space for the kids to be kids and space for me to put the pieces back together.

I used my intuition and trusted it would show up at the perfect time, even though I ended up living at my mom's for a week. It worked. Better than I could ever imagine.

My intuition felt like a voice – check the rent website now. There it was. Still detached from the outcome – I contacted the rental agency. Appointment was set. It all came through with ease. A boat load of surrender and a heart filled with trust.

Re-write

I spent a ridiculous amount of time searching for the new home. Mostly out of fear instead of waiting for the intuition to guide me. We all do this. We take un-aligned action which relates to burn out and fatigue. When we feel this, we are going the wrong direction. We spend SO much mental energy on the what ifs. Not seeing that the answer is right in front of us if we would slow down and pay attention.

We get stuck in our mind trying to figure it out. When the easy path was always within us. Using our built-in guidance system. To trust that even if the answer doesn't make logical sense – it will in time.

Journal it out!

- What are you waiting for to ask your higher guidance for help?

- What do you want?

- How are you getting in the way of it? Paying attention to the lack of it?

  Pushing it away with fear?

- Start out my manifesting something meaningless like an incredible front

  row parking spot. Something you won't lose sleep over thinking about it.

- THEN your job is feeling good. Only see the things that make YOU happy.

  Happy manifesting.

"As you are shifting, you will begin to realize that you are not the same person you used to be. The things you used to tolerate have now become intolerable. Where you once remained quiet, you are now speaking your truth. Where you once battled and argued, you are now choosing to remain silent. You are beginning to understand the value of your voice and there are some situations that no longer deserve your time, energy, and focus." Unknown

Above all else. Choose you. I promise you your soul will jump for joy. You will FEEL it inside. Do the work of looking at what is going on within. Your inner game is reflected externally. I can't repeat this enough. It all starts and ends within us.

Decide you are worth. I believe in you!

Light Your Soul on Fire

Finding your TRUE Self

One of the best most costly lessons I have EVER learned thus far. Self-love is a daily practice and when you take a couple days, weeks, months off you will see it in all areas of your life. I had a vision and a message on my heart that was really starting to create an incredible form. I found my purpose. Or it found me. I was on a mission to find and help others that have depleted souls like I did and show them the tools and paradigms that they could shift to REALLY start living the life of their dreams.

You know that girl sitting on the kitchen floor with tears rolling out of her eyes. Looking around wondering what she did wrong. Yes, those people. I feel their hearts and the solution gets to be sweet surrender.

I remember the day vividly. Standing in front of my bathroom mirror. I was reading frantically about self-love and one of the tools was to look yourself in the mirror and tell yourself I love you. But the truth was. I sure didn't love myself. I cried. How was I ever going to convince myself that I even liked myself?!

Day after day I continued the practice. Within a couple weeks I started to notice a change in how I felt – mostly about myself. I made lists and lists on what I loved about myself specifically and over time the list grew.

We all came into this world perfect. Authentic. Raw and real. And then the world gets ahold of us with the best of intentions. We layer up on layer junk on us that doesn't serve us. And then we turn 30ish and realize we are a hot mess. We have never been taught how to love ourselves and that – that is even a thing.

You can be, do, or have ANYTHING you want. The caveat: I cannot serve unless I am authentic. Nobody can create me. I get to BE me.

"If you keep avoiding self-love, the universe will keep sending people who also avoid loving you, hoping you get a little clue." Unknown

Your relationships are mirrors of what is going on within you.

You are in control.

Learn from your mirrors. Heal the wounds you are carrying around.

Love yourself hard! ❤☒

You have enough.
You are enough.
You do enough.
You are love.

Re-write

You are meant for great things. You are one in 400 trillion to be born the day you were born and be the beautiful person you are! YOU DON'T EXIST anywhere else.

Journal it out!

- What do you love about yourself?

- Where could you release the comparison to others?

- How can you love yourself more than you do now?

- Are you willing to stay laser focused on you and your relationship

  with you to transform the relationships in your life that are less

  than mediocre? If so... ask your guidance system like this:

Spirit/God/Angels/Soul what would you have me know about my

relationship with myself? Where can I focus to improve?

"Sometimes the right path is not always the easiest one." Unknown

Love note to you:

It's all perception.

We tell the story that it is hard... when we don't want it to be.

We don't realize that it is the story that is making it hard. Not the actual event.

Pay attention to the story.

Journal it out.

Then decide. Is this REALLY how I want this to go?

What will you lose in releasing the story?

Resentment? Struggle? Anger?

What if you let it be easy? Put down your resistance and allowed yourself to CHOOSE ease, flow, peace, love?

Much love.
Becca

Light Your Soul on Fire

Teachers

Letting it all out today. Feels SO good!

Striving to be better. Raising my vibration - but damn! I am headed to go to the gym today. I haven't been there since the spring. I am in MUCH better shape. I have transformed into a pretty incredible human in the last 6 months but the old vibe sets in. I am not enough. Judged. Nobody will like me. I am weird. I can't make a darn friend there. Maybe because I am awkward. Like being a round peg trying to fit into a square hole. I just haven't really fit anywhere I entire life. (Probably why I tried so hard to fit myself in a mold for SO long.) Just to be accepted. When all I needed to do at such a young age with accept myself.

I walk into the gym. The journaling in the hours prior of HOW this was going to feel. (Reminder that we desire things based upon how they will make us feel – not on the ACTUAL desire.) I felt it all – and being in the gym for the first time after deciding how it was going to go. Was.... Well incredible. Exactly how I journaled it to go. Felt amazing!

Now this 'process' is no band aid. I still continually do the work every day before I go. I feel welcome. I feel included. I feel those that felt like the round peg and I embrace them. I have turned what was once a dread into a feeling of family and community. I decided. I showed up. I wrote the story. I felt the feelings ahead of time. And then I surrendered and walked through the doors.

Did you know - the teachers that present itself in your life are there to test the upgraded YOU. To build the muscles that you have created as you increase your inner fire. Growth has never happened with roses and candles and light music playing in the background. We need resistance. Old stories to come to the surface. Old people to show up expecting the old us. Resistance shows us how to get to the new vibration the higher consciousness AND hold it. To go higher. To up level like you have never up leveled before. Find inner grace for the resistance. See it for what it is. You asked for it - now let it teach you.

"Your life gets better when you do. Work on yourself and rest will follow. "

Show up at the gym (or wherever you wrote a story of despair) after you have re-written the story of how this is YOUR place too. The old energy has dissipated. I am honored. I am welcomed. I am re-born as Becca aka gym rat. Or not but you get my drift. Re-write that shit. Feel into how you want it to go. Then surrender to this or something better.

Today when I walk into the doors of this incredible gym – I am greeted and feel welcome. I LOVE the energy. The people. I am building incredible relationships. Making lifelong friends. Becoming more accepting of myself and my body in the process. Falling in love with myself and my life in a deeper way.

A year ago, this experience was totally different. The change? Was my story. My perception. My lack of love turned into love.

"Peace of mind comes piece by piece." Yogi Tea

Re-write

Any area of your life that seems to feel less than – try this out for size. How can you re-write the story to make it how you desire? Be patient and present in the process and watch the magic unfold.

Journal it out!

- What is one area that you are disappointed in? An area that is

  preventing you from greatness?

- Write out the story and why you are disappointed?

- Is this true?

- What are you making it mean?

- Where have you put meaning into this story that may not be completely true? Just your perception?

- How do you want it to go instead? Journal it out in detail. Can you feel it? Can you feel as if you are already there? It going the way you desire? Now hold that energy every day and allow it to unfold... like magic!

Love note to YOU:

The way to shift anything on the outside is the shift and heal on the inside.

Forgive.
Release the story.
Write a new one.
Love yourself.
Accept yourself.
Heal within.

Be willing to see it differently.

Re-Creation

Unbelievable I thought. You mean ALL that I ever knew isn't real? I am living in the Matrix? I was taught low vibe is life.

The gift of resonance showed up. Like smacked me in the face. I was sitting in a living room and someone was talking about Angel Numbers and I was like um what?! Just so happens they see Angel Numbers. Something felt good about it, but my ego was like REJECT REJECT REJECT. I believed in guardian angels and I feel 'presence' on occasion but what the what?!

Low and behold 1 week later.... Numbers started showing up over and over and over again, 111, 222, 333, etc. Constant numbers all over the license plates, signs, the time, and then I decided to go down the rabbit hole. Angels speaking to us via numbers. I found a great site and book that shows the messages of the angels. They were SPOT ON! The guidance was out of this world. Ha! Literally! The messages were exactly what I needed. Exactly what I was asking for. A crazy coincidence via numbers.

The more open I am the more they speak to me with different signs. Those I have introduced to the angelic guidance start to see them quickly after our conversations. Always beautiful words of encouragement and direction that speaks to their soul. Total resonance.

Retreat after spiritual awakening after synchronicity, and repeat life REALLY started to look like a dream! A DREAM!

I started to see how with I was creating my life and the guidance was giving me the easy button. I went from crazy burn out WEEKLY and messed up hustle to the beginning of SUPER flow. Because hustle - that is how you achieve everything right?! Working hard is something to be proud of. Look at what I created?

NOBODY says wow that was easy?!? AND you created that! Great job! Doesn't exist. My demons and stories of how could this possible be arose. Self-doubt soaking my bones. But I was SO tired. I wanted to just get 'THERE' so I could rest. I mean I am only worthy if I have a list of accomplishments rights?

Do ALL the things. Have ALL the things. BE all the things.

Perfect parent. Dream home. Hot hockey mom ride. Career that makes people gasp. Incredible vacations. Beautiful skin. Saying all the right things. Changing the world in a way that is corporate approved. Dressed in a way that says - she has it all together. Clean home. Oh, come on.... This list is depressing. Even when I read it again. Did I REALLY want that?

It was ALL the thing's society says is incredible but never aligned with my soul and my heart. So, I let it ALL go. I quit caring about other thoughts and started to care more about how I felt. What I desired. What worked for me. Let's be honest - other judgments will never allow me (or you) to be happy. So, let's toss them out right here at this very moment. Let's decide. Decide for it to be done. Decide to let go of all the beliefs that got us into this mess in the first place.

Then I met Abraham Hicks... and Bob Proctor.... And then Tony Robbins... and many other amazing teachers and I took the pieces from each that resonated. P.S. Never believe everything you hear regardless of who you are learning it from. Resonance is ALIGNMENT. ALIGNMENT is YOUR personal path. Don't veer off your path in a mere attempt to get to where you want to go faster.... It will prolong it. Trust me.

Side note: Let's dive into this thing called resonance. It is when you hear something, learn something, experience something and it FEELS right. Almost like you knew this but didn't know you knew this? Ok good. You are with me. Your TRUTHS will stand out with resonance. Pay attention. If your body rejects it and it feels like a should.... DON'T DO IT. It's not your path.

Your path feels good. It feels like an exhale. It had NOTHING to do with how others are doing it. Trust your internal system. EVEN if the top teachers in the world are saying this is HOW it is – listen to your guidance.

Ok off my soap box.

So, with all these incredible puzzle pieces I looked at my life and made a list of what is going well, how it happened, what isn't working, how that happened... AND it was TRUE. My beliefs were either creating or destroying what I desired. Like SOUL-level desires in complete alignment with WHO I am at a soul level. Deep meaningful things.

IF you are the creator of your life and everything you think consistently becomes true.... What are you creating?

Journal it out!

- What have you created that you are ready to shift into something better?

- How will that look?

- Where in your life are you not following your internal guidance system?

- Where is your guidance system leading you to now?

- What does your soul want you to know?

Light Your Soul on Fire

Waking up with 'THE' Hangover

The hangover of societies crap. Writing this book was part of it. I keep getting hung up on how a book should be written. I fall under ZERO stories of how things should be done. Society sure has taken a hold on me. As I actually let it. Not knowing that if it doesn't feel good and/or work for me - I am not doing it. Not now. Not ever.

The hangover was rough. Blood shot eyes. Lifeless body. No amount of nutrients was going to bring me back and three little kids looking up at me wondering where I went. I hustled. I achieved. I scrolled Facebook to see what others were doing and improved that area in my life over and over again. I did ALL. THE. THINGS. Except cooking. I never honored that.

When I allowed myself my to fall into the stories of what success looks like by studying all the people that have gone before me that have massive success, AND THEN tried to do what they did. UGH. It didn't work. I did it over and over again and the only story that came up. Success at that level was never made for me. The money. The body. The man. The family. The career. Society kept yelling at me - If you do it my way then you will achieve. So, I did it OVER and OVER again.

Do you watch what others are doing and mimic them?

I remember the day I made the decision out of PURE fear. Fear that I would never make it. At this time a single mom determined to make ends not just meet but give my kids a life worth living. Whatever that meant at that time. I had mentors in my life that said IF YOU DO THIS. Then your life will forever change. Now you may feel regret from me, but it was one of the most beautiful lessons of my life. Lessons after that fact that shoved EVERY SINGLE SOUL out of my life that I kept around for FEAR of FAILING. They were my.... If they are here, then I will succeed.

Bullshit Becca! Oh, it was SO out of alignment. Filled with fear. I was SO angry for so long. It took me MANY forgiveness ceremonies of writing and burning to release them. To set myself free. TO see that they were only there to teach me that my true power was already within me.

I didn't need a strategy. I didn't need to follow someone else's success path. I had to unravel ALL of it. And fall into deep and beautiful alignment. And surrender ALL of it. Let it go. Allow God to lead. My intuition to speak up. The howl the sweet sound of my soul. To get back onto my path of Joy, Nourishment, Peace, and all I ever wanted at a SOUL LEVEL.

Love note to YOU:

Strategy doesn't work.

IF it did. Everyone could DO the strategy and they would all get the same results....

YOU can over and repeatedly try different methods that work for others and STILL hit the failure button.

It is because you are tapping into OTHER'S gifts. They achieved because it was THEIR gift. Not yours.

Take your eyes OFF the others. Go inward. Tap into YOUR gifts and get to where to want with EASE.

Hustle was NEVER necessary. Hustle comes from fear. Fear of not enough. Once you connect. Plug in. Get the inspired action. Take the action.

FIREWORKS.

Bigger and more beautiful than you have ever experienced!

Journal it out!

- Where are you not honoring yourself?

- Trusting that you have all the answers within?

- Trusting that you will be guided to exactly what you need to move into the

  next level of your life?

Riding the Vibe

I was sitting at church one Sunday as the pastor spoke about one of his favorite topics, elk hunting in Idaho. Nothing I was interested in, but it got my attention. He dove deep into the understanding of why this certain man had an 80% success rate but everyone else had 5% rate if that. When he questioned why the gap? He came up with an interesting concept that sunk right into my soul.

Immersion. 80% success rate only comes with 'ALIGNED IMMERSION'. A soul calling followed by immersing yourself into it EVERY day.

It is like our body. We can't work out for 3 months and get good tone and then quit. Just check it off the list and move on. It is a lifetime immersion of showing up daily and doing the work. The same goes for our vibration. By now you realize the vibration is the key to success in all soul led desires. Hold a higher vibration get a better result. Play the vibe game well and life looks and feels pretty darn good!

High vibration feels like – euphoria. It's a choice. A choice of showing up every day and seeing the blessing surrounding you. It is seeing the good in others. It's OK to feel down, sad, mad etc. Just don't stay there. We feel it to heal it and then we let the vibration raise back up. You are a high vibrational being at the core. Meaning that there are layers of crap crowding the REAL you. The one that had vibrant energy, and a passion for life. I see you there. Trust that it is there.

I decided to take a great group of souls through the process of holding them accountable for an immersion into a higher vibration by kicked off the layers and shifting into the seeing the world through a different lens.

I led a 30-day immersion course that CHANGED. MY. LIFE. To pour into others but it forced me to show up every day and shift perceptions. To make the choice. Not to mention the beautiful souls that joined me. I was feeling SO high that I never stopped after 30 days. This course is on crazy awesome repeat and many new souls jump right in every 30 days!

What I learned: When you are always constantly in awareness of your vibration. You can shift it faster and avoid the dips that sabotage the very desires on your heart. Your feelings are an indicator of the direction of your vibration. Just stay awake. Stay aware.

Today I woke up feeling like I was going to cry. Waking up from a dream of a tornado coming and I was teaching my kids how to harness themselves in this shop to protect themselves. Mind you these little people are age 4-7. My vibe was a mess. I felt empty. Lost. Confused. The lowest I have been in a VERY long time. What created this? How did I get here?

All poor questions. I shifted to... what does my soul need right now? A nap was the answer. Feel all this emotion - as resistance strengthens it. So, I felt it. The ugliness of all of it. Then I fell asleep to a meditation playing on my phone. I could have worked out. Called a good friend to talk it through. But my soul said sleep. I honored my soul as it KNOWS the easiest path. Easy is not lazy. Easy is efficient. Easy is super flow. Easy is shifting into an incredible life in moments instead of years.

Your vibration can shift when you process what is – by journaling it out and burning it. THEN, asking your soul what it needs. Doing the thing. Moving along.

I was stuck in writing this book for over 6 months and it all flew out of me after I woke up. My soul knew. Knew I was ready. Knew the world has been waiting. Knew it wasn't about me. Knew it was my time to shift. I listened and followed the guidance. It has never left me astray.

Re-write

My soul only knows the way to my highest vibration. It knows what I need for nourishment. It knows the exact person to talk to, the activity to do, the path to achieve all that I desire. I choose to follow it above all else.

Journal it out!

- Where am I falling asleep in life? Falling asleep at the wheel of life?

- What are activities that feel super incredible to me that improve my life?

- Is PLAY included in this?

Love note from me:

Play.

When did you decide that play was no longer a part of your life?

When did being 'grownup' trump the joy of your soul?

What did you make it mean?

Who relayed the message to quit acting like a child?

Play is an expression of your soul.
A vehicle that fuels your most creative talent and gifts.
A feeling that amplifies the ability to manifest quickly.

Your job is feeling good.

Light Your Soul on Fire

Success by Starting Over

I was not by ANY means confident. But the message was coming through my soul. I kept having the 'feeling' if I could share my lessons and ah ha moments with the world. My shifts. My success. My awakening. All of it. I would FEEL freedom. It was in me. Being bottled up. I wanted SO badly to let it out, but I just couldn't. An 'expert' came into my life for this beautiful lesson and found a way to monetize my madness. I didn't care if I got paid – I just needed a platform to let it ALL out. So, they set it all up. Created a plan and executed.

The 'problem' was I kept changing my mind. Adjusting. Shifting. Really actually evolving at a rapid pace. I couldn't stop and saw so many beautiful inspired ideas. None of which really got to where I was visualizing them. Like a dandelion constantly spreading its seeds. Allowing the wind to blow me exactly where I needed to be.

The problem. I wasn't confident. I had never hired anyone before. I trusted someone else's ideas and judgements. I asked for permission. I allowed someone else to create the plan. It didn't feel right but I trusted. I ignored my soul and allowed my ego to fuel my path. My ego loved the story she painted. The gorgeous website. The products that I had no access to. I had no control – but my ego allowed it to continue because it felt like I SHOULD do this.

It ended up COMPLETELY crashing. I was heartbroken. Stuck. Money lost. Time lost. And REALLY nothing to show for it. Have you had moments like this? Moments or years of failure. All of it a wash. Or did you find the silver lining.

See I learned THIS: Your soul only knows. There isn't a single person in the world that can communicate your soul in an authentic way like YOU do. The brand was always me - not a creation from an expert. Real. Raw. Authentic. Bumpy. Clumsy. Unpolished. On fire. Random. Passionate.

I never needed a beautiful website. I needed ME. The unadulterated version of ME. I never needed a plan. I needed to ask my soul, WHAT IS MY NEXT STEP? WHOM am I serving today? And then follow the guidance.

It took me lots of bumps and a SERIOUS lack of confidence in what my soul was whispering to me all along. See the soul is very respectful. It is nothing like the ego. The ego yells - gets in your face, but not the soul. The soul comes from pure love, pure innocence. A little whisper when you listen, and you will hear it. You will hear what you need to know in this moment.

When the crash of my ego. All I thought I was coming to a grinding halt. I came to a place of serious surrender. I thought I had a plan. But really who's plan has ever worked. This brought me to my knees. I just prayed for an answer and it was SURRENDER. As Abraham Hicks says - just flow down the river Ms. Becca. Throw the oars to the shore. I was never meaning for this to be hard. This lesson was vital to me learning what raw and authentic really is.

Weeks later I was back on my feet. Ready and able to see in the eyes of total surrender. I built a website from scratch. Put together a 'brand' which is still not a cool color scheme or anything fancy. I never will have someone make it LOOK better. It is whatever my soul decides to create is all that it will ever be. Real. Raw. Authentic. Soul led creations.

I started to create from a place of love. Products. Courses. Whatever felt good. Like an exhale. And then I started to step out more often into the light of the social media world and speak my inner message that was attempting to come out of me. It felt good! Scary but good. Super scary. Fear of rejection lying underneath the surface. What is the alternative to not allowing my authentic thoughts and transformation to be shared? An empty soul. I will never allow my soul to empty again so I jump. Every day.

I needed some intuitive guidance. I needed to understand my inner message. I needed to find someone that was doing what I desired but had truly found her 'super flow'. I hired a coach. A coach that was SERIOUSLY next level. She was intense. She was the soul level version of herself that my soul yearns for. A serious badass that I couldn't stop following. She blew me away! My soul cheers every time I work with her and make another shift, another up level.

She was the push to become the leader I came here to be. To show beautiful souls like you that you already have everything within you that need. Nothing, I mean NOTHING outside of you will ever give you the level of abundance, joy, and peace that you desire like your soul led life will. I dare you to follow it. Trust even when you can't see the next step.

Re-write

I believe in me. I believe in anything that comes through me from my heart. I allow my soul to speak. I decide and choose every day to be authentic. I am worthy of living the life I desire on my terms with no rules.

Journal it out!

- Where are you allowing your ego to guide your life?

- What does your soul REALLY desire?

- If you KNEW that your decision would be embraced by the world – what would you have, be, and do?

- What did this trigger for you?

- What areas do you see need additional growth?

- What stories from the past that may have debilitated you are you still holding on to that are stopping you from Being the best version of you?

Light Your Soul on Fire

Burn the List

I did it again. I created a to do list from the inspired action steps I was given from the universe. But then I didn't act in that moment. It turned into a list. It FELT HEAVY. A weight on my shoulders. I even wrote some of it on the whiteboard. So ugly inside. I felt nauseous. Controlled. I threw myself out of alignment even when I KNOW the laws of the universe. Take the action when it is given to you.

I burned the list. I released it back to the universe. I questioned why I would go there when I know better.

How many times have you made the list? The list that governs your life – that feels like a prison. The one you can't get away from. It keeps growing and we start to perceive that time is becoming less and less. A FEAR that continues to grow and grow until we hit burn out and a level of unhappiness that we didn't know we created.

The list – fueled my ego. It gave me a sense of accomplishment or, so I assumed. I read all the self-help books (ok - not all of them) but many and how to make the list work and how to move it to the next day etc. I made myself silly trying everyone else's methods. I bought the best planners that had the hourly calendar and I started to schedule them into my calendar like priorities.

The issue – I have kids. You know those kids that could care less about schedules. Yes – I have 3 of them. Anger, resentment, and frustration continued to build. I was disappointed in myself every time my head hit the pillow at night. I was pushing my kids further and further away. They would ask me to play and I had another to do scheduled.

I thought I would get SMARTER and schedule in time with my kids. Talk about a joke. They were never interested in following a schedule to play with me. My list turned into controlling my life based on a fear of not getting the 'important' tasks done and keeping my life in line.

What I didn't see was that I was following other's strategies instead of just asking my soul – how do I do ALL THIS?

I burned the list. I no longer make ANY lists. I journal like it is going out of style with anything that comes through me – but ZERO list making. You are probably wondering how I am surviving life?!

It is called TRUST. Knowing that I am divinely guided and that everything that needs to be done (not defined by me but by my higher self) will get done. I will get to where I need to at the right time. I just follow my inner feeling, voice, nudge, etc. Remember it is a whisper... so meditate for 5-10 minutes a day or more to tap into this guidance in a more profound way.

Side note: If meditation is hard for you to sit in silence and BE with yourself. Be ok with that. I was there for a VERY long time. Light an organic soy candle (because fragrance in candles is super toxic and I care about you) and then watch the light and set the timer on your phone or just focus on your breathing and how your body feels. Allow yourself to BE. You will start to get ideas, messages, etc. once you quiet your mind. Allow thoughts to run through you like clouds passing by. This is no time for perfection my friend. Some days will be good, and some will not be. Whatever it is. Show up for you.

Schedules and lists may take us to being out in the future which fills ourselves with anxiety and worry. None of those that you have time for. We are operation enjoying life so being present is our number one goal. Meditation will build your muscle for being present.

What you can schedule. Self-care. Time with your soul. Time to journal. An incredible morning routine that makes you feel like a million bucks every day. They exist. It's up to you to find your groove.

Here is what I do... I allow this to be fluid and change when I feel I need to:

I schedule out time to do my purpose work (the path directed by my soul). Less time that I think I need as we always fill the spaced allotted. I do high vibrational things for my morning routine: meditation, journal, and get myself in a confident energy. I work out almost every day earlier on in the day. I go to yoga multiple times a week to assist me in surrendering and being present.

Re-write

I can effort out life OR I can let the universe do its part and just stay in a state of super flow – just flowing down the river.

Journal it out!

- Where are you attempting to control your day?

- Where could you release the EFFORT and follow your inner nudges?

- How would it FEEL to accomplish more, align more, all while flowing with

  the day?

- How can you let this more into your life?

Light Your Soul on Fire

Fear

Fear that I wouldn't do enough. Fear that if I didn't do MORE I wouldn't get to my desire. You see 34 years of programming created this. It can jump out of your cells of your body in a moment. The feelings of lack. Of not enough.

My mantra became as this moment. I am enough. I have enough. I do enough. And I took a nap. I let it ALL go. I released ALL of it. My projects. My love. My family. My home. My friends. My income. I surrendered it all. All that I was starting to grip to. I asked my guides to turn up the heat. The heat of my soul.

Fear has a funny way of popping its head into our lives. A way of manipulating the life we want versus the life we currently have. We look at what is in front of us wondering why we are still unhappy but afraid of making any changes.

Fear blinds us. It turns off our intuition and puts us in a state of fight or flight. This can turn into depression or anxiety if not paid close attention to.

We were headed to a hockey game and I was feeling irritable AGAIN. It seems that was my choice of emotion most of the time. Not knowingly. But the rest of the world knew it. I jumped on the resource with ALL the right answers – google. And I googled this... Why do I feel irritable ALL THE TIME? Well I found a couple interesting things – one being that depression doesn't need to feel sad – it can be one of anger and irritability. What do I have to be depressed about? I have everything I desire and manifest new desires pretty darn easy. I knew this had nothing to do about stuff. I dug deeper. You never know where google will lead. I felt divinely guided to go there anyway.

Consistent feelings of irritability and anger with is FEAR with passion is the underlying feelings of powerlessness. It slapped me in the face. Where do I feel powerful? Not in my parenting. The kids desire control and freedom, so I feel most of the time I have very little power. 3 little kids against mom. In my relationship – I don't know where it is headed. I don't believe that marriage means that there is stability in any relationship – statistics show this. Today is it good but what will tomorrow be like? How will I know that this will last? That this will work? My purpose work and the work of my soul – every day is something new and I never know where it is leading me. I am for sure not in control there. I can't control the amount of sleep I get – puppy and little kids and sometimes my thoughts keep me up at night.

I was feeling a spiral out of control and it produced excessive yuck feelings within me. All of which I was projecting on the rest of the world.

The tipping point: I wasn't trusting the process. I wasn't allowing myself to remember that I created ALL of this. Good and bad if we want to judge it. The judgement being mere perception. My focus sucked. I was looking at ALL the things I didn't want AND telling the story about how hard, bad, frustrating, etc. it was. I was letting my fear get the best of me.

I allow myself to follow my guidance BECAUSE it works! It guides me to more profound beautiful results – more amazing that I could dream of. Just by trusting, asking for guidance, and taking inspired action.

Listen to your voice within. Life become magnificent when you trust it. But be ok if you sometimes revert back to fear. It is a dance and there is no perfection in this journey of life. It is the continual remembering of WHO we are and WHY we are here.

Re-write

Trust. Trust that when I take the next step, I will be perfect guided, and the step will appear. The universe will never let me fall. It was never my plan – it was always his. Allow him to lead as he knows what is best for me. Stay in my heart. In a state of gratitude. Stay present. My power is in the NOW... this very moment. When I revert to the past of what was (depression) or the anxiety and worry of the future I surrender my power and BECOME irritable and angry. It is a choice. I choose joy. I choose presence.

Journal it out!

- Where do you feel powerless?

- Where is you focus?

- How can you surrender my plan and trust and listen more intently?

- What could you implement daily to help you stay focused on being

  present and trusting the process of life?

Love note to YOU:

Asking for advice is only helpful IF you felt guided to ask.

Never because of self-doubt.

You have everything you need within you.

The direction.
The answers.
The inspiration.

What if this year you decided to... TRUST yourself?

Light Your Soul on Fire

Alignment on Steroids

My favorite part of this whole process. Type A personality waking up each day without a plan. My whole life was based on a process of the successful. The morning routine. I shifted into asking the questions first - what does my soul need right now? What is my next aligned step? A single step that creates MASSIVE quantum leaps. Allowing the universe to do its part. To work in harmony with a much bigger power. My intuition and soul guides and when I feel like I am SUPER disconnected my angel guides step in when I ask, and they relay the messages I need to continue the path.

My world changed when I found alignment. We all have different things that take us in and out of alignment.

What I have allowed to bring me out of alignment:
Kids not listening.
My love not paying attention to me.
People not answer the phone when I call. (I know lame right.)
The puppy peeing on the floor as she is headed outside.
When I am really cold.
Messy house.
Scrolling Facebook and watching others highlight reels and comparing myself.
When I gain weight and my pants don't fit right.
When I get cut off in traffic.
When I have to wait.
When my truck is not clean.
When I am nervous and doing something for the first time.
When I forget something.
When the kids make a mess.
When the kids are super loud and running around the house.
When something gets broken.
When I feel disorganized.
When I procrastinate.

Do you see a theme here? Almost anything can take us out of alignment IF we allow it. Most of it is ridiculous – IF I allow myself to judge it. It is our HUMAN. Beautiful and flawed all in one.

What is it for you?

You see the ego feels the need to control the world around us. To provide us optimal safety and if we allow it – it will take over our life and keep us in a state of mis-alignment. The exact place that caused us to manifest health issues (more in Louise Hays book – How to Heal Your Life), financial issues, relationship disasters, poor parenting, and how we show up in the world in a low vibrational way. We don't want any of this so why do we create it? We are the creators of our life you know.... Perspective and perception are just the thing to turn this from and ego and fear focus to a heart issue.

Side note: Many times, triggers and mis-alignment can come from childhood events that are still playing out well into our adulthood. Notice this. Check out the journal questions below to dive in deeper to see if it stems from something within that needs to be healed.

Kids not listening: Deep breathe – how can I connect with them and understand what is going on within them and why they can't hear me? What are the facts? What am I making this mean? Am I making this about me? Am I playing the victim?

My love not paying attention to me: Is it someone else's job to continually place me at the center of their attention. Um no. When I find myself being filled up by someone else actions then I KNOW that I am forgetting that I have everything I need already within me. I shift back to filling myself with love and attention instead. Our closest relationships are our biggest teachers.

Not answering the phone when I call: Same as above. Allowing everyone else off the hook of needing to make me happy and doing alignment for them. Which may mean not answering the phone if they do not feel like it. Again, what was I making it mean? Rejection? My stuff, not theirs.

The puppy peeing on the floor: Lacking love and compassion. Going deeper – where am I withholding love and compassion for myself? When I shift this to providing it for myself, I no longer need it externally.

Feeling cold: Looking at the glass have empty and feelings of lack instead of the gratitude of what I do have. The ability to warm up etc.

Messy house: Same as above. It's a story. I can function in any situation with joy and love and ease and alignment. It's a choice. We choose our emotions. The home is lived in and loved. A clean house doesn't not MEAN anything. What am I making it mean?

Comparing myself: Lack of self-love for myself. Denying myself the very love it needs. Comparison is by far the thief of joy. We can't compare apples to oranges. NONE of us are the same. Trusting I have the skills and abilities and that I am perfectly created the way I am.

Gaining weight: It is my bodies way of getting my attention. To see it. To honor it. TO start taking better care of it. I also learn to love myself regardless of what the number on the scale is. The scale is meant for me to pay attention to it and give it the nourishment and love that it desires to feel whole and complete.

Getting cut off in traffic: It is a mere judgement. When I judge others and allow my shadow side to show – it is because I judge myself. Again, another projection. How I feel about others is REALLY how I feel about myself. Time to do a reality check. Am I unconditionally loving of myself?

When I have to wait: My time is more valuable than others. What if the universe was stalling me due to divine guidance – to protect me or to guide me closer to a human or such that I have been manifesting. Again – trust the process. That at all times I am at the perfect place at the perfect time. Time is an illusion.

When my truck is not clean: Mere judgement. I am only worthy if I show the world cleanliness. Shifting this to – I am worthy and always doing the best I can with what I have. (I mean 3 kids riding around in my truck all the time... it is bound to get dirty sometimes....)

Nervous doing something for the first time: I allow the lack of confidence to at time self-sabotage something that felt so aligned to do. Believing that I am in a partnership with god and the universe. This isn't all me. I am only the messenger. When I shift here it is easy to release the nerves and trust what will come through me is perfect and divinely guided.

When I forget something: Hello human. Your expectations of yourself may be a little ridiculous. Shifting back to I do the best I can with what I currently have. It also is a great awareness of maybe I am a bit ungrounded and unfocused. Then re-center myself.

Kids make a mess: Back to my beliefs that step around being clean. I am worthier when my life looks clean. Says who? Who are you trying to impress Becca? What happened to play and joy? The mess is just a part of life and is to be embraced.

High energy noise and activity: When this triggers me, it is showing me that I am lacking on self-care. I look for what is going on under the surface. The trigger is usually never the issue. What haven't I journaled or processed to be released?

When something gets broken: I usually see the dollar signs that I am creating lack mentality. I forgot to trust that financially I am always supported. Anytime we feel financial lack we are attracting more of that into our lives. (More on this in the bonus section.)

Feeling disorganized: I picked up a belief somewhere in life that if I am organized THEN I will be successful. It pops up on occasion. This appeases my striving personality of doing something and feeling productive. I organize WHEN I feel guided – WHEN I need to create space. Otherwise I usually just free fall.

Procrastination: I find this funny that this brings me out of alignment. What procrastination is: Doing something that is not in alignment with who you are, what you need, and your desires. It is a message that there is a better more aligned way. Yes, laugh away.... We all do it.

"If you accept a limiting belief, then it will become a truth for you." —Louise Hay

What brings me INTO alignment:
Both sides are especially helpful to know but this list is GOLD.
Hot tea.
Working out.
Sauna.
Deep conversation with friends.
Afternoon naps.
Reading a good book curled up on the couch.
Learning something new.
Advancing my skills.
Helping someone see their life in a brighter light.
Connecting with an old friend.
Playing with animals.
Being out in nature.
Meditation. (This one brings me into alignment the quickest).
Taking a walk.
Cleaning.

An organized closet.
New clothes.
New socks!
Being an observer of life.
Choosing a state of surrender.
Being present.
Sleeping kiddos.
Fresh air.
The lake/ocean.
Travel and adventure.
Music.
Journaling. (This is the second fastest way to get into alignment)
Massages.
Getting my nails done.
Drinking green veggie juice.
Taking my supplements and essential oils.
Fresh flowers.
Gratitude.
Watching my kids try something new.
Yoga.
Creating something to help others.
Early morning reflection.
Crystals to raise my vibration.
Sage to clear negative energy from my space.
Palo Santo which creates good energy.
Focusing on all the things I love and that are going well.
Approaching life with unconditional love and compassion.

Re-write

As the creator of my life. I get to decide. Alignment or not? I am in control of this always.

Journal it out!

- What pulls you out of alignment?

- What the focus in each of these instances? Heart or Ego centered?

- What puts you into alignment?

Releasing childhood triggers:

- When was the first time you felt this in your life?

- How old were you?

- What was happening?

- What did you make it mean?

- Now embrace this emotion. Where do you feel it in your body? Allow yourself to feel ALL of it. Do not resist this. If tear flow let them out.

- Now embrace yourself with unconditional love. Embrace this younger version of you. Tell them that you love them. Fill them full of the emotions that they desired at that moment.

- Now re-write the scenario how you would have preferred it would have gone. Allow yourself to visualize and FEEL how this would feel. Replacing the old memory with the new one. Reprogramming your inner computer.

- What is going on under the surface? Sometime journal dumping is helpful. Let out everything onto paper via pen and then rip it up and throw it away. This takes the low vibrational energy out of you and releasing it back to the universe. Creating space within you.

Love note to YOU and confession time:

Truth is I struggle being a mom. It doesn't come natural to me at all. I would rather work, create, clean, read a book, explore the world....

Why? Because I can control me. I can't control them.

They have been my biggest teachers. Constant surrender. Releasing expectations. I struggle because I think it should look a certain way (society's beliefs), act a certain way (belief from my childhood) ....

None of these beliefs were ever mine. They were shoulds I picked up along the way. Other ideas.

The truth is- I am only their guide. To help them develop their souls so they thrive in their life. To help them to be mindful, and heart centered. To keep play as part of their everyday life for all of their life.

Where did we get all of these ideas of how this is supposed to be? It has been miserable trying to keep up.

I am releasing the old energy of overwhelm, disappointment, frustration, and confusion - to energy of understanding, love, patience, presence, and laser focused on connection.

I am going to BE with them instead of constantly doing. I am going to focus my energy with them and hear them.

We never teach by what we say. Always the example we set by our actions.

I am grateful to continue along the path of awareness to BE better and continually assess and up level all areas of my life. Today it is being the 'next level' mom.

I've got this and so do you!

Stay awake. Pay attention. When we shift so does the rest of the world.

xo

Becca

Turning up the Heat

What does the next level you look like? Feel like? Think about? Do for fun? LIVE like? These were all questions I began to start asking and journaling on. My biggest shifts came in the form of journaling out whatever came up through these questions. Then imagining how it would look. Then asking my soul what it needs and then what I need to know. Talk about crazy incredible transformations. Letting go of all my shit and creating space for the life I REALLY desired. One where I can allow my voice to reach millions in a message of encouragement, and message that shifts you to see the world and your life in a different way, a message of love.

The heat can create a lot of crazy ass fears. Let me tell you about mine.

You see I grew up in what I would define as a strict catholic family. Both parenting attending catholic school as kids. Going to church was mandatory every Sunday. I am grateful for having this experience as a kid as it really helped me figure out how to connect with my higher source as an adult.

The process and craziness of the way the Catholics did God really never clicked for me. It was not my cup of tea. I believed in unconditional love – and totally acceptance. The rules just didn't work for me. The separation and judgement did not align with my heart. (By no means I am saying that there is anything wrong with this denomination – just sharing my experience – as always YOU DO YOU.)

The day I moved out of the house I quit going. I eventually found a church that was non-denominational and much less churchy. It fit but as you know with my personality, I grew out of it within a couple years. Church was fine. I believed in God. I knew there was a bigger power working through all of this but still craving something deeper. I wasn't getting it from church.

I ended up making friends with a great group of 'wo-woo' friends. You know the incredible spiritual type that you can't quit asking questions to. I had such a deep resonance to SO much of what they were saying. I felt hope. I felt a connection that really was indescribable. I was starting to feel whole again. My soul was cheering and jumping around within me. A sense of understanding coming through me.

I love talking to others with different styles of belief systems. See I believe in love and love doesn't judge. Not ever. Especially when it comes to individual belief systems. If someone is moving towards self-improvement, love and understanding – that is a win for sure!

Fast forward to more recent I have been posting my spiritual insight into the internet and the social medias of the world and well the 'bible thumpers' are after me (or at least the ones that are judging and are unaccepting of my messages). The religious focused ones. The ones I have always been afraid of disappointing. They are not liking my view points. That I speak about the universe. You see I believe that everyone gets to go down their own path of resonance. What feels best to them. My 'job' is to question if it what they or anyone internally are called to or if it a belief of someone or something else that they are just living out. This is just what I do because that is what I was taught, OR this is what fuels my soul.

Religion and spirituality head off here. I don't believe in a set of rules. I believe in unconditional love and compassion. Never segregation. I believe in the way Jesus walked the earth in the stories - always seeing people as whole. A higher consciousness that is SO rare. I believe that we all came here as souls in choice to learn and grow here on this spiritual playground. I believe that each of us are in charge of creating our life. It isn't God giving you the upper hand or the lower hand. It is the role of the victor not the victim. Regardless if the bible is true or not REALLY does not matter. (This may be a potential trigger – beliefs can separate us forcing judgment and making us compelled to force our beliefs or prove something to others that do not believe the same as us.) What matters is it is a great book that has some incredible wisdom in it. Wisdom if it feels good to you can lead you to a better life. ONLY if you are called. YOUR soul always knows. Nobody else does. Trust it. Release the judgment of yourself. I may not need to attract those that judge me in my attempt to show a perspective that might just spark something in other souls.

Always– you do you. If it resonates within you. Explore it more. Peel back the layers of societal programming. God is love. That is all. Universe and God can be interchangeable – unless previous beliefs have taught you otherwise. What is YOU and what is 'others beliefs' that you are carrying around? How do you know? If it FEELS good continue that path – if it doesn't go into exploration of what is out there. There is a path here for everyone.

Re-write

Life is about finding out WHO you are and what lights you up. When you are next leveling your life, you can serve more, give more, love more, open your heart more....

Journal it out!

- What triggered you?

- What resonated with you?

- How can you allow yourself to view the beliefs that come up and be

  OK with questioning them?

- What are you making it mean?

- Where can you instill more love and compassion into your life with

  yourself and your world?

Light Your Soul on Fire

Self-Sabotage

Truth is you will do it. I will do it. The INTENTION is to be aware WHERE we are self-sabotaging the things we desire and shifting them. Sabotage can be a gift to show you what is going on under the surface.

Self-sabotage is neither good nor bad. Yes, sigh of relief. It is only an indicator that something is going on under the surface.

We may believe we are self-sabotaging something when in turn we are only turning away from what is no longer in alignment with who we are. OR we have an underlying belief system that is preventing us from going in the direction of what we desire.

"Remember: We all get what we tolerate. So stop tolerating excuses within yourself, limiting beliefs of the past, or half-assed or fearful states." —Tony Robbins

What is self-sabotage? It is not following your inspired actions. It is turning away from your soul. It is ignoring your incredible gifts. It's allowing the subconscious beliefs to take over. It's choosing perceived pleasure over perceived pain. It is numbing ourselves from the 'stuff' in life that doesn't feel good.

Self-sabotage can sneak up on us in crazy odd ways. Get this...

I am doing my thing. Working into being more authentic. Following my soul. Stepping up and out from the shade of the tree. Allowing myself to be seen. Underlying feelings of discontentment getting heavier and heavier on my shoulders every day. My thoughts upbeat. My focus – always positive. Consistently moving forward. My vibe – dropping.

Diving into the work that I teach trying to find out WHY I am going backwards when all the 'signs' point to success. What is going on under the surface? Why am I not able to manifest with ease like so many others? Why do I feel so stuck?

I was stuffing my pain. I was turning my head when I saw something I didn't like and focused on the positive. The problem was it was triggering my fear of abandonment and it was rearing its ugly head to be healed. I had deep work to do. I was numbing myself with positivity. A different kind of drug. I was numbing myself with a smile when I wasn't feeling anything that allowed me to smile. I was avoiding and self-sabotaging everything – all to avoid pain.

We make choices based upon pain vs. pleasure. It is the story we tell about it. Healing and feeling a childhood wound is incredibly painful. Seeing it. Allowing myself to go back to childhood when I made my Dad's actions of going to work mean something. I made it mean abandonment. It hurt my soul to feel this. The story needed to be re-written. It needed to be released.

My next and newest form of self-sabotage came up through focusing on the short-term gain vs the long-term effects of my choices. The good old weight gain tactics. I realized I have been doing this for years. I can gain weight quickly and I do when EVERYTHING else in my life is going amazing. I feel accomplished when I fix a problem. Mine OR someone else's. So, I created a problem of weight gain to solve the problem with losing the weight. It works. I am good at it. Like a roller coaster. I was only focused short term versus what the swings were doing to my body and my health long term. I got to redefine accomplishment. I redefined it as how I am being during the day. Being present. Being in the moment. Staying in my power. The only place to get the power we all desire is in this very moment. Keep your thoughts here. Your soul here. Your body here.

Many numb themselves in other ways – medication, drugs, alcohol, food, positivity, shopping and spending, gambling, and there are probably a lot more. What do you DO to feel good? To numb the pain? Who do you turn to? How do you avoid it?

For the 20 seconds it takes to sit in the pain of the past and FEEL all of it. Pay attention to where you feel it in your body. Define it. What does it feel like? Hold the attention and the focus on the pain and watch it dissipate. We must feel it to heal it.

Re-write

You are worthy of having it all – create space by letting go of the stories and events of your past. You deserve it all! You deserve to be in the energy of healing your pain. Allow yourself the unconditional love you desire.

Journal it out!

- What do you desire?

- Why would you decide NOT to have this?

- What do you believe about it?

- What actions do you do to sabotage your desires?

- How can you re-write these actions to be a source of pain instead
  of pleasure?

- How can you release and forgive the other humans involved in
  your perceived pain?

Inspiration with love:

Will I do enough?

Will I accomplish all I desire this year?

Calm down. Listen.

Do you hear the guidance?

You don't have to do it all today.

Be present. In THIS moment.

Your power is in the present.

Surrender your plan.

Show up every day and ask for your next step. Take massive action.

Trust.

This or something better.

Allow the universe to do its part.

You are not alone. Nor do you need to do this alone.

Affirm your desires. Let them in.

Take a deep breath.

THIS or something better.

xo

Becca

Your Soul Only Knows

The exact same energy goes into manifesting an amazing life vs. a life of just enough. What will it be for you?

I have sat in the energy of both. We have a natural tendency to feel all lit up when we grow and when that growth feels like competency. When we accomplish and check things off a list from that competent energy. When we decide where it is that we want to grow and have control over our growth.

We tend to fall off our rocker a bit when growth comes from the unexpected but very necessary lessons for why we are here. Death, divorce, break ups, fired from job, sickness, relocations, car accidents etc.

I've done it all. The Steven Covey way of organizing your life. The Dave Ramsey of getting the finances in tip top shape. The Chalene Johnson perfect push planner to get it all accomplished in less time. I read all the books, *5 Minute Manager*, Success Principles, 4 Hour Work Week, Jack Canfield's array of life success etc. The matching stylish outfits. The matching socks. The organized silverware drawer with the silverware perfectly stacked. The couch cushions arranged perfectly inspired by pottery barn.

I thought to BE successful I would need to look the part. Hair on point. Do videos. No interruptions in the videos. Act as if. Outfit flattering. Good lighting. Read all the books so I would KNOW what I need to know to BE the person I desired to be. AND... be seen as the person I wanted everyone to see.

Successful. ✔☒
Have it all together. ✔☒
Happy. ✔☒
Organized. ✔☒
Influential. ✔☒
Certifications. ✔☒

All ego shit. Al society programming shit. All jaded beliefs. All exhausting...

What if we were ALL authentic? ALL living a life we love based upon our INNER guidance. Think of how amazing this world could be. Honoring others. Never comparing ourselves... because for real we are 1 in 400 TRILLION. We don't really have anything to compare. You are an apple and I am an orange. We may both look to be round aka human but that it is. That is the ONLY common ground we walk on. We were born with incredible magical gifts and no two are alike.

9 months into an AMAZING relationship. One I manifested. He was like a unicorn. Exactly what I needed to grow, the freedom I desired in a relationship, and an amazing influence on my kids.

It sounded crazy. Society was yelling at me that this WAS NOT a good idea. People in my life were questioning my decisions. Who moves in together after 9 months WITH your kids?
I asked my gut. My deep-seated intuition that practically yells at me now with answers WHEN I ASK.... Is this the right decision? Is this my next move in this game life or chess? Is this too soon? Is this good for my kids? Is this too fast?
My intuition was a hell yes. YELLING at me. Do IT!

Trust. Living in a deep state of trust. See I had experience with crazy unconventional guidance prior going through the divorce and ALL the steps through the ending of the marriage to know that all I needed to do was LISTEN. Then TRUST.

Imagine steps in front of you, but you do not actually see them. You pick up your foot, possibly hesitating and still seeing nothing – and then you step. MAGICALLY a step appears if out of nowhere and for sure not what you envisioned it to look like. More beautiful, more stable, and more supporting that you have seen ANY step – in. your. life.

That is what I have experienced. So, when my intuition says move in. WITH your kids. This will be great. This is what you desire and SO much more. I trusted it. Blindly really. With NO idea what was in store for me.

Looking back over the last years – it has been perfect. The perfect growth that has strengthened our relationship. You see people come into your life for a reason, a season, or a lifetime. It is NEVER up to us to know which one it is. We just stay present, heart centered and stay in a flow of continual growth and awareness. Keeping OUR cup filled up and overflowing. Two people constantly paying attention to themselves and growing themselves creating a pretty profound deep relationship – intimate or not.

I don't regret any of it. I am glad I didn't listen to what society or others said and had 100% complete trust in my guidance AND followed it. I live here now (in a DEEP state of trust). It is beautiful and sometimes un-nerving. You just never know what is next and something crazy can turn into amazing or better than amazing. (Like my beautiful car starting on fire…. That is a story for later in this book…)

Re-write

Everything is ALWAYS working out for me. I TRUST that nothing is good or bad – it is just what is. I listen to my inner guidance ALWAYS and follow it KNOWING deeply that it is always leading to my desires. THIS or something better.

Journal it out!

- Where are you ignoring your soul?

- How do you know when your soul, spirit, your higher self is guiding you?

- Where have you felt guided to in the past where you didn't follow your inner nudges? What was the outcome?

- Where in your life have you followed the nudges? What was the outcome?

- What fears come up about following the guidance? Where do you feel hesitant to trust?

- As you journal out the fears. LOOK at them. Are they real?

- Start with the small things – like what to eat? Where to shop? Where to park?

- Allow your intuition and your soul to guide you. Be sure to set intentions in advance. Practice builds your trust. Enjoy the journey.

Letting the Spiritual Guides IN

We all have guides, angels, higher self, God, ascended masters, etc. guiding us within this lifetime that speak to us in ways that we understand to help us navigate to growth, adventure, and experiences in this lifetime. The word used to describe may be different for everyone. Find what RESONATES with YOU. Resonance is truth and everyone's is different. Trust your own. Go with what feels good.

This part of my journey is where I would listen to others having experiences with something bigger than themselves and I was intrigued but still had beliefs from childhood that made me question if this was all ok? God are you listening? Is this ok? Is this right?

Deciphering between beliefs and our inner truth can be some of the most resistant work we have here on this earth. See I grew up Catholic. I was given a list of what to believe and what not to. I just followed it blindly for many years just doing what I was told – but it never resonated. Now there is nothing wrong with religion and following a set of beliefs – it just wasn't jiving with me. Inside I felt something more. Something based on love and compassion. With Jesus as my role model. He was all up in the love and compassion. So, anything regardless of rules, religion, beliefs etc. – THIS is how I started to find my truth. Was it love and compassion, and if the answer was YES, I headed that direction. If it was division, unloving, separation, war, fighting, being against something, I was out. Not going to do it. Not believing in it. It made releasing beliefs that weren't mine easy. Does it feel good? Nope. Ok bye Felicia. Like picking weeds. Out with what doesn't jive.

The spiritual guides were just the cherry on top when it came to my life experiences going forward. Giving me deep incredible clarity and moving me TOWARDS more love and compassion towards myself and others.

I sat down on the floor – angel cards being strewn across the carpet. Intuition guiding me to select the cards based on a feeling in resonance to my questions. What's next? What would you have me know? What does my soul desire for me to know, do, grow etc.?

Angel cards. Also known as tarot cards, oracles cards – they are all little different. Obviously – only pick out a deck that feels good to you EVEN if it seems a bit off and you are still in the judgement of them. It's OK.

I cannot believe STILL to this day how accurate the message is. It is a super easy way for me to move ahead with confidence getting the exact answer needed even if sometimes I did not like it. Like when it points out my shadows – the dust in the corner of the closet that I am not interested in looking at.

One reading it came up with the harshness I was exhibiting towards my children and the guidance was one of really it was the harshness towards myself that needed to be healed. When I sat with it. Looked at it. Felt it. Forgave myself for the way I spoke to my children and myself. My parenting improved. IMPROVED. All from something that I thought was not ok and that people only did at renaissance festivals. Like playing pretend and guessing your future. Which I learned was SO far from the truth. Even cooler that I could do it for myself. Trusting myself AND my guidance.
So today. Sitting on the floor. What does my soul want me to know?

Before I tell you what they said... Let me give you the back story. This weekend (Today is Monday) we went on a fishing trip 5 hours or so to northern Minnesota. I have never been, so I really didn't know what to expect.

Friday night we get to the fish house that we will be staying and sleeping in and as we are unloading one of the seats had gotten very hot and STARTED ON FIRE. I mean flames coming from my Denali. My most favorite vehicle I have ever owned. Up in flames. We had no fire extinguisher just below zero weather and a ton of snow to try to put it out. Crazy right?!

I have been super calm and trusting that everything will be fine but honestly inside I am worried. Will I need to get a new vehicle? What really went wrong? Thankful our kids were not with us. Thankful it didn't happen until we were parked and not going down the road. It has been a bit traumatic for me and all while I need to process and feel my emotions, I also need to trust that everything will work out amazing. How can I allow this to be effortless WITHOUT putting in ideas of how I think it should go best? SUPER FLOW.

So, the guidance: "*Stop worrying. Everything is going to be fine.*" Is the first one I get. Funny huh?!

This is a kind universe, and everyone within it is working in your favor. There are no tests, blocks, or obstacles in your way, except your OWN PROJECTIONS OF FEAR into your future. Take a moment and hush your mind, quieting it from worries and fears. Feel me brush your brow with a new energy of faith, hope, and optimism. These energies fuel your exciting present time, as well as all future movements. Why would you wish darkness upon yourself when light shines all around you? Step into this brightness by lightening your thoughts and feelings. You must stop worrying, as this anxiety squelches the goodness that seeks to find you! Clear your heart of fear and replace those energies with ones that will serve you and your family instead. REFUSE to think of anything except your bright today and tomorrow, and I promise you that it shall be so.

Doreen Virtue Goddess Guidance Oracle Cards

This is breath-taking and life giving REALLY. It is funny how they mention family and I sit right up like YES family let's go!

How am I projecting fear into this situation? Looking at all the what ifs? Running the many scenarios in my head. I shift instead to gratitude. NOBODY got hurt. It is just stuff. Stuff can be replaced. Everything is working out for me.

Re-write

When I allow the guidance in, I can make the necessary adjustments to my thoughts and feelings and allow life to be effortless.

Journal it out!

- Where in your life are you PROJECTING fear on it?

- How can you allow your guidance to calm those fears?

- What beliefs inhibit you from hearing and allowing your guidance to come

  to and through you?

Feel it to Heal it

When life gives us lemons, we make lemonade- WHEN we remember. Sometimes we forget about the lemonade all while starting blankly at the lemons. Life is full of so-called heart breaks. The events that wrench our souls and break our hearts into many pieces.

Out of nowhere it can creep up on us. Never realizing that we created the lemons via our fears. Letting them keep us up at night focusing on the wrong story line. The story line we never wanted to happen.

I woke up. Wiping the sleep out of my eyes. Peering out the window to see if the sun was planning on blessing me again. Not knowing what they day would hold. I am learning to set the intentions in the beginning of the day so that they creation of this day may never happen again.

We had plans to enjoy the summer day.

It started all wrong. Fueled with manipulation and ended in heartbreak. A story that instead of flow we choose force. We had expectations that turned around and bit us in the ass. We reacted instead of responded. We could have just altered our plans – walked away. Surrendered to a higher source. We pushed on with the vision of how it should go in our head. All while it is blowing up. Right in front of our faces.

We may never know why. It is really none of my business, but this happens to all of us at one time or another. We project and create pain. We are so engulfed in our pain that we can't shift our energy to get out of it. We hold onto the pain – because of what we fear we will lose if we release it. It manifests in our bodies as dis-ease. If we hold it for years or decades, it may even turn into cancer. Cancer is just a manifestation of long-standing resentment.

We hold on so dang tight to the way it ought to be. The way it should be. The story and picture of our head not realizing that what we desire is a culmination of the beliefs, thoughts and feelings oh and stories that we project on our external world. Our outside circumstances are a reflection of what is going on within. This event clearly showed it. We tried SO hard. Instead of surrendering and trusting and listening to the guidance within. Damnation at its finest. If it's hard we are ALWAYS headed in the wrong direction....

It's ok. We ALL do it. It is a lesson. One that maybe we should avoid repeating for a lifetime. But still a valuable lesson. When we feel the pain of regret. We can CHOOSE to hold it blocking the energy flow of the body or we can let it pass through like a stranger walking by in Central Park. When energy get blocked and we grip to it like our life depends on it everything that comes behind it jams up – like a nasty traffic jam.

We want MORE. But we CAN NOT manifest from this space. We cannot dwell on lack of ANYTHING and receive. We must let go. Surrender. FEEL peace within even when the outside world is anything but peaceful. Allow ourselves to FEEL nourishment. Let the universe fill us up. Let God in. In whatever way feels good to you.

Once we FEEL the pain, we can release it. Lean into it instead of stuffing it down. It will not go away – EVER. Unless we feel ALL of it. The discomfort. The agony. The regret.

This is HOW I release the junk holding me down.

I write out pen to paper ALL OF IT. How I am feeling and anything that needs to come out of me. I sit with it. Finding WHERE DO I FEEL THIS IN MY BODY. Leaning into that feeling. Letting any emotions come to the surface. Journaling it all out. Until I have nothing left in me. Then I burn it or rip it out. Removing the energy from me.

My FAVORITE part is next. I get out a crisp white blank piece of paper. I ask myself – what would I create instead. Shifting the energy. Allowing the solution to come to the surface. Releasing ALL limitations – waving the magic wand. I FEEL the new story. The new way. I feel the relief come over my body. I ask my guides for the next steps. What would you have me do next? How would you have me look at this? I may use angel cards. I find understanding in the new way. I CHOOSE and DECIDE to heal this. That all now is well. That my power is in the present.

Re-write

When something arises to heal, I choose to look at it so that I am not spending decades learning the same lesson. I allow my soul to guide me through it. I sit in my shit and feel it as I know the rainbow always comes after the rain. Healing creates space for a better life. This all teaches me to be a better co-creator.

Journal it out!

- Journal out whatever comes up with this.

- Where in your life does the energy need to shift?

- What will you create? Today? This week? This year?

Deciding HOW it will Go

Your TRUE AUTHENTIC power is hidden in a decision. Deciding what energy, you will step into. What level of YOU. How you show up in the world is based on a decision. Getting your confident energy behind you and backing yourself AND your dream FULLY.

It takes the exact same energy to stay stuck as it is to decide and up level. Which do you prefer? Stuck is telling the same story all while getting the same results. It is sitting in the same energy and feeling the victim story. It is allowing yourself to play at a level that was never for you. (If you are feeling resistance and self-doubt around any of this.... That is ok. I am great with triggering you. Triggers is how we grow. Sit in it and allow yourself to work through it.)

I don't wake up every day confident. Neither do ANY of my mentors... like EVER. We have all learned how to get into the confident energy.

You wouldn't recognize me 5-6 years ago. I was toxic. Really toxic to myself and it was mirrored in SO many of my relationships. I was in a pretty deep relationship and the verbal abuse was imminent. I would never let anyone else speak to me the way they did. I felt and told the victim story – it was a broken record of how they always treated me poorly and I came up with a ridiculous number of stories on the daily to prove it. My focus was hard wired into the victim. I benefited from the attention I got from it. It made me feel loved when people wanted to hear about it.

When we lean into toxic it is partially because we are benefiting from it in some way. It strengthens the story we tell about why we are not where we desire... it gives us the attention we desire from one of our parents when we were a child... or a gazillion other semi-logical reasons.

My story was good. Everyone in my life knew the story. Half of it was probably posted on the Facebook. We can get this way easily if we are not paying attention. If our awareness meter is on low. If we check out of life. If we are lacking love for ourselves and searching for it from anyone and in anyway, we can get it. Even if it is from playing the victim card.

The awareness set in. It was painful. My mentor showed me point blank that he was just a mirror. We only allow others to treat us the way we treat ourselves. We set the bar. We create the standards. At minimum I was ripping myself apart on the daily. Believing the story that criticism was to strengthen me and to enhance my accomplishments in life. It was cutting me apart piece by piece. I was beyond critical of myself. I judged myself and at the rate I was going I would NEVER be enough. I was never the victim of anything. I was the product of decades of mere drips of self-love and TRUCK LOADS of self-hate. It radiated in my life in ALL my close relationships. I was critical of EVERYONE. My ego – in full control. Helping me to feel safe by projecting my shit upon anyone that got close to me.

The beauty of all of this was the awareness. I wasn't about to enter another relationship with this level of toxicity. Life would be better alone. The relationship I craved wouldn't succeed because... I was bringing myself with me. So, anything that came up in this 10 years of growth would seep into every relationship going forward UNLESS I DECIDED to heal it. All the drama. All the rage. All the disfunction.

I remember the day vividly. I looked into the mirror (because the book told me to) and told myself OUT LOUD that I loved myself with my hand on my heart. I BAWLED. Like a baby. Ugly cry. Hives. The whole deal. I didn't believe it. I didn't actually feel this way. I felt like a complete failure. Divorced mom of 3. I had nothing. Who would want this? My self-esteem at an all-time low.

Self-esteem is a decision. We either believe in ourselves or we don't. We either stand up or we sit down. We do the work every day to continue to believe... OR we don't. It is a decision.

I decided to stand up. If not for me than for my kids. I decided to tell a new story.

Re-write

I decided that I will love myself more than ANYONE else. I will fill my cup to overflowing. SO, I can be the SOUL the world craves from my family, community and around the globe. I decide to maintain my connection and to let God work through me. That I would be the vessel. I would deliver the message that I was created for.

Journal it out!

What will you decide?

How will you show up?

What no longer is serving you?

What are you no longer available for?

Light Your Soul on Fire

Finding the Triggers

I am in the middle of a coffee shop boutique. It's right before Christmas and we are searching for the perfect gifts. This place is BEAUTIFUL. The people. The ambiance. I turn around and I can't find a single kid of mine. My heart drops. The underlying fear sets in that has come up in past experiences. It does NOT feel good. Panic sets in.

I am getting these feelings, these triggers with my kids a TON lately. I am honestly getting sick of feeling this way. I feel like a victim sometimes to crazy kids. I know though after much of my spiritual practice and understanding that I am not really the victim. It is something from my childhood that needs to be healed.

That evening I allow myself to spend time in meditation re-living my past. When did I feel this deep-seated emotion in the last 5 years? Late teens? The first time I felt it?
The event came rushing to the surface. I was young. Maybe 4 or 5. Maybe a little older. I was outside playing. I lived in 5 acres out in the middle of nowhere. Maybe 5 or 6 cars would drive down the dirt road in a day. I remember this day vividly. I didn't have many toys, so nature was my entertainment. Who knows what I was really doing?

A car drove by going faster than most cars. Two males started screaming out the window. It was mid-summer afternoon. It was probably just a couple of kids having fun.

It scared the life out of me. Small little child – not knowing or understanding what had happened. The same feeling from the coffee shop. Radiating through the cells of my body. 35 years old and I STILL feel this event that I would have never guessed related to my feelings of fear today.

From that day on – my entire childhood I would hide behind the LP tank ANYTIME a car drove by. Repeating the fear response over and over and over again.

When we go to the first time of feeling a certain emotional chain and heal it. It releases all the events that occur after it. Releasing it from the cells and tissues of our precious bodies. Releasing the discomfort and pain that has set in and triggered throughout the years.

I haven't had this fearful feeling set in since. How beautiful to heal a trigger from childhood? How beautiful to move forward and to feel deeper feelings of happiness within just with this little exercise of looking at the trigger and going backwards.

I forgave the boys that were having some fun on a beautiful summer day. I forgave myself for making it mean something. I released it to the universe to turn the energy into something positive. I set myself free.

Every time I or one of my private clients are triggered, we go through this same process. We release it FOR GOOD. Pick the weed and move on.

Re-write

A trigger is just an indicator that there is something that needs to be healed so it doesn't manifest into dis-ease within the body. I am worthy of feeling good. I trust that I am always supported in FULL by the universe.

Journal it out!

- Where in your life do you need to take a good look at what is triggering you?

- Can you go there? Can you feel it? Can you journal it out?

- Where do you feel or experience dis-ease in your body? Check out Louise Hay's book "How to Heal Your Life." For detailed thought patterns that relate to what is manifesting physically in your body. She is pretty rad.

Shoulding on Yourself

When your body/intuition/internal nudge says hell no – but you FEEL you should. It is such a slippery slope. WHO are you trying to make happy? Does it enhance your happiness? Does it fill your cup?

Who are you walking on eggshells for?

We teach people how to teach us based upon you honoring you.

I was looking externally for the answers and doing ALL the things instead of looking within. I needed someone tall dark and handsome. I needed it to LOOK good. Going against ALL the things I was feeling.

We were driving to get our engagement pictures done. Fighting the entire way. It was hard to even fake a smile for the pictures. It looked perfect. By this time, I had completely suppressed my intuition. I was numb. Forcing this all to happen mostly for fear of being along. I had many along the way question my choices. It made me mad. I painted the picture and I was damn sure it was going to go exactly the way I wrote it. I had ZERO trust and I was going down this road alone.

I am extremely grateful. LIKE EXTREMELY grateful for this experience. To have such strong intuition to the point of praying that this feeling would go away so I could go through with these plans. We got married – when all the signs were pointing to no. He was the perfect person for the perfect lesson. Walking down the aisle I had already known that backing out would have been painful. More than honoring myself. He knew it too.

It doesn't matter the decision. The money poured into it. The effort and time invested. You ALWAYS know. If you decide to listen. You will hear it, feel it, and be drawn in a certain direction.

THERE IS NOTHING TO FEAR. I mean use common sense but take risks. This life is short AF. Go there. Do that. Be that. Feel it all. We came here to experience this all. Acknowledge the gifts and growth from the many lessons you have already experienced. LEARN from them so you are not continually hitting the repeat button. Falling on our face is part of the journey. Pushing through because I SHOULD. Because it looks good. Because I don't want to be along. It was all a beautiful storm.

We are built upon the stories of our lives and it strengthens us and inspires us to dig deeper within us we can't find the answers outside of us. The answers were never external in the first place. Like Pink's song – Beautiful Trauma. Such is life. Find the silver lining. If it's hard you are going the wrong direction OR telling the story that it is hard. Let it be effortless. Let it fuel you. Let it allow your soul to burn brighter. I teach others BEFORE they go through it. To heal yourself AND others.

Imagine. Any relationship.

Asking someone to do or be something else for you – for you to be happy. It doesn't work. It builds resentment. It destroys relationships. It lowers the vibe. I did it. For years. I still sometimes do it to my kids. Expectations are toxic. Projecting our needs on others is toxic.

Lean In. When you need something externally – find a way to fill the need internally. Give yourself more love, more attention, more self-care, more adventure, more intimacy, AND THEN.

ONLY focus on the good things you LOVE about the other person. Create harmony with your thoughts and feelings all while filling up your tank.

Re-write

I honor myself as #1. I honor others in their journey. No judgement – no asking them to be different. Just loving them unconditionally for WHO they are. With no strings attached.

Journal it out!

- WHO are you trying to make happy?

- Does it enhance your happiness?

- Does it fill your cup?

- Who are you walking on eggshells for?

- Who is walking on eggshells for you?

- When have you not followed your intuition and it resulted in a regret where

  looking back you knew where you were guided and went against it?

Light Your Soul on Fire

Surrendering it ALL

In January of last year, I had another midlife crisis. Another plan I made that was being shifted by the Divine. My heart feeling broken. Another loss of a dream. I keep thinking: OK, I am on my path and this is how it will look. Making plans. Forgetting that nobody ever has plans that work the way they were written. I asked for BIG things. WORLD impact. SOUL work. Stepping into my purpose.

I asked that my primary income become team driven so I could step aside and UNLEASH my soul to the world. Raw, Authentic, Real. Nothing polished like most of the world. I wanted SO many to see that they already have what they need. The message on my heart SO FLIPPING BIG.

I was guided to step away from growing my current full-time income as a holistic health coach. I was no longer feeling fulfilled and I knew I desired more but SO much guilt came up over me. My plan was to go all the way. My vision was so strong. Everything was just coming together.

What I forgot is that I asked for this residual income to fund what was coming through me. Imagine sitting in a world of creation without having to worry about how the bills will ever get pain. That was where I was but STILL upset. My dream was shifted. It was time. Time to surrender it all.

The lifestyle, the relationships, the family, the career, the life plans. Lay it all down before something much larger than me. I meditated for days it felt like. I cried. I begged, and then I allowed.

I allowed the message to come through. It was time for the world. I was as ready as I was going to get. It was time to show my soul. My truth. The love and compassion that I was creating within me.

I took the leap. It was choppy. My vibration was super choppy. Some days confident and some days on my knees wanting to hide. For fear of what I would say, create, post would offend someone. But then again who ever walks through the world without someone not approving or liking what we do. It doesn't exist. So, speak to those who need you. Show up. You will always be provided for. Let it all go and listen. The ride is more beautiful than you can imagine.

Re-write

It's never our plan. Let go and let God.

Journal it out!

- What are you gripping to and pushing away in your life?

- How can you stay more in the moment instead of wondering what is ahead in the future AND trust it will be amazing?

- What specific things can you do to surrender daily?

- What stories and expectations do you realize you are still gripping to?

Love note to you:

I believe that everything happens for our growth. To break open our heart. To increase our compassion. To surrender our plans and allow life to unfold. To release our stories and expectations.

To love. All things teach us to love.

See the lesson. Surrender daily. Allow magic to unfold. Trust that you are always supported.

xo

Becca

Creating Space

Your closet is clogged with old clothes that you might wear someday. Clothes that hasn't been touched in years. The smaller size that when you lose the weight you can wear again. The larger size just in case you gain some and need some nice clothes to wear. Maybe it is organized or maybe its complete chaos. Organized by color and type or just put where-ever you can find space. There is an energy to this closet. There is energy within this clothing based upon the emotion behind it, where you bought it, when you wore it, who gave it to you, etc.

Do you remember what it feels like to clean it out? Release the stagnant energy. To let go of the torn and tattered pieces you have been hanging onto for years?

This stagnant energy is not just hiding in your closet. It is in the essence of your life, your beliefs, your home, your stories, your relationships, the places where you spend your time. It is an energetic signature.

When we are in the process of up leveling and next leveling our life and stepping into the energy of WHO we now decide we are going to be – we MUST make sure there is the space required to do so.

How do you bring your soul mate love into your life when you are sleeping in the middle of the bed, your closet is packed, your schedule is packed? How will there be any energetic and physical space available for them to enter your life.

There is an overhaul that needs to take place when we desire to bring something new into our life. It may be mental, physical, emotional, spiritual, etc. How will you receive the guidance from your spiritual guides when your mind is cluttered with social media, tv shows, what is going on in others' lives etc. How can you achieve a deeper relationship when you are not willing to make space in your emotional life for them to enter at a level you desire?

This was me. I was afraid to open my heart completely. Afraid of relational failure. My emotions were completely cluttered. I loved him more than anything. The pain of failure still looming in my past. I desired more than anything to let him in, but my heart was mostly closed. The thought of being vulnerable was painful. It is not the same process as cleaning out the closet.... Or is it?!

The emotions and stories tied to physical objects are the same process when it comes to emotional clutter. To achieve a truly intimate relationship – I got to let go of the stories of how it would be hard, it would be painful, I would get hurt again, it is working well right now where we are at. If I allow myself to create space to let him in to a deep part of my heart that very few have ever been in – it will be hard AF if it doesn't work.

But I came here to this earth to LOVE. To LIVE life in a way that inspires others. While still hiding my heart. I feel the tension in my heart as I write this. Just like creating physical space in our homes (that FEELS incredible to do) it isn't a one-time gig. We need to do it consistently or it will get cluttered again. Same goes with the heart. Why was I making this hard???

Because of the perceived pain I may experience if it breaks. Emotions have a way of preventing us from living our best life because of the contrast.

The truth is – there is not dark without light, sunrise without sunset, rain without the rainbow. We are here to experience it ALL. I can't possibly believe that I can walk through the rest of my life without heart break. Without the deep-seated pain of loss. Loss of a person, relationship, a dream, physical tangible things that have strong meaning in our life. The full spectrum of feeling is really the joy of life.

We can't appreciate happiness if we have never felt sad. We cannot appreciate joy if we have not experienced anger. We cannot understand the powerful effects of the deep feeling of love without experiencing heart break and picking up the pieces that have shattered all over the ground.

My beloved truck ended up getting totaled this last weekend and the emotions I felt of loss over something that REALLY has little meaning in life. I got attached, as so many of us do. I felt – as we are all emotional beings. It is(was) a beautiful storm. I decided to get a car as the rental vehicle in the interim of finding a new truck.... AND wow did it make me appreciate the stability of the truck through snow and ice and the feeling of security a larger vehicle gives me. We need to experience contrast in our life to solidify and/or show up what we REALLY desire on a deep level. Even in something as simple as the vehicle we drive.

Growth isn't always happy and enjoyable. It can be some of the most 'painful' experiences we have but looking back some of the most amazing lessons. Adopting the this soon will pass – paid is never forever understand lets us sit in it as we are cleaning the proverbial closet of life.

Re-write

I can have all my desires as long as I create the space to let it in. I am worthy of having it all.

Journal it out!

- Where do you need to create space?

- What is cluttering your life?

- Why are you not allowing your desire to enter your life?

Love letter for YOU:

We all have a choice.

We can flow down the river with ease or we can paddle upstream and create a life of constant struggle.

What if.... you could have a life you LOVE, and it was EASY?

Enough is enough. You are ready to find a better way.

Without the rules.

Creating a life you LOVE!

Done worrying about money.
Done wishing your health was better.
Done wondering if your relationships will ever get better.

Or if this is just the way it is.

The everyday cycle of going to a job you don't love. Feelings of stress and anxiety. Done with burn out. Survival. Going through the motions.

Actually achieving.

Instead of letting yourself down. And letting the doubt and fear take over.

You KNOW you are ready. YOU CRAVE alignment. A life that feels good.

More than just on a vacation or the weekend.

Ready to FEEL....

Abundant
Ease
Flow
Full
Laughter
Joy
Love

You are READY to see this WHOLE life thing differently. YOU ARE READY to SHIFT!

If you are....

Ready to surrender all that you know.
Do the work.
Trust the process.

YOUR life will change FOREVER.

You will step into a role of BEING. Being the creator of YOUR life.

Living a life BETTER than you can EVER had imagined!

YOU are WORTHY! You are DESERVING!

The next level.... is WAITING for you!

Allowing your Soul to light on FIRE

It always starts with you. What you believe. How you decide to see it. Let it be easy. Hit super flow. Be happy. It's a choice and an internal game.

When you decide to allow your inner flame to burn bright – it starts with authenticity. Giving yourself the permission to unapologetically BE yourself. Others can FEEL when you are coming from an authentic energy. Developing and becoming more authentic everyday by removing the beliefs that do not serve us and following our inner light and passion creates a life we FALL IN LOVE with.

It started with a decision to allow us to BE unapologetically ourselves in TRUE authentic fashion. Speaking our truth with every step we take. You can have all of this. The question is...will you allow it? Will you let it in?

I believe in you. I believe in you because I believe in me. Promise me you will back yourself fully. You will lean on number 1 – YOU. You will go ALL IN. Everyday show up and share your gifts with the world regardless of the likes, shares, comments, thoughts, etc. SHOW up. The world needs you! Fan your flame and radiate the light within!

"Never be afraid to live your life boldly.
Dream big.
Ask for what you want.
Believe you are worthy of having it all.
Release attachment.
Expect miracles to appear."

Light Your Soul on Fire

Bonus: Your Money & Your Mind

How we relate to money directly affects the success of our life. I can't not talk about this forbid this be blocking you. Not acceptable. Let's knock it out of the park.

Did you know that the money that runs through your life is directly affected by the relationship you have with it? The money you attract and the amount you keep. Money is just an energy. Just like everything around you. You are either attracting it into your life or you are pushing it away. You have conscious and unconscious stories about money that are directly impacting your results. There is a distinct difference between the energy of making money and keeping money.

Step into this energy of abundance with me. YOU are a trust fund baby of the universe. Abundance is FEELING. It all comes with a decision to show up every day and FEEL the feelings of abundance. Focusing on what you have and all the amazing blessings showing up every day. When you start to lean towards lack you create more lack. When you view money in a negative and fearful way – it takes up your energy and it is draining you from doing what you came here to do. To live the life you desire to live.

Money is not good or bad. Good people do good things with money and bad people do bad things with money. What is your intention with money? Why do you desire for it to show up more fully in your life? The desires of your heart are placed on your heart by God. They are YOURS. You can have them.

Money responds to your energy and your belief system. Once you drop the limiting thoughts and stories that you are telling about money and to money abundance rolls in without crazy effort. The work is in monitoring your thoughts that come up as you buy stuff.

I started flowing with my money. Not really balancing my accounts but always trusting that there was enough. It was like playing roulette with my debit card. I had no budget. No idea how much money was coming in or going out. It felt like freedom. I didn't want any restrictions in my life including in my finances. The money seemed to drop in at the perfect time in the perfect amounts. I had a super flow going on I thought. Looking back, I am not sure what I was doing. Probably creating another great like lesson.

The month came where it ALL blew up on me. I ran out of money. Completely. I freaked out. I had to instantly put myself in a state of surrender. God what would you have me do? I totally prayed like crazy – I trust you. If I learn the lesson right now in this moment will you guide me to turn this all around?

I have never been so ashamed at the moment that I would allow myself to get into this situation but HEY – I'm human.

I spent time journaling this all out. The whole mess. Soul what do you want me to know about this? God doesn't give you more until you take care of what you have. I believed I was taking care of it. When really, I was treating my relationship with money foolishly. Money just like any other person is a relationship. When you haphazardly go into a relationship without an intention or a desire you may get what we will call a SURPRISE.

The answers that came through my journaling and letting my higher-self speak to me, was that I must respect the relationship, pay attention, be present, and it is up to me to tell the money where to go. Setting intentions for how I desired it to show up in my life.

You see. I have a bachelor's in finance degree, I worked for an incredible insurance company, I worked hand in hand with some of the best financial advisors, I had gone through Financial Peace University, read many of the top financial management books and yet I still failed. It is NEVER about what you know. It is about what you do.

I believe in transformation. Information does nothing but store up space in our brain. Transformation is the real gift. So, I headed down the part to truly figure this all out.
There was nothing to figure out. My relationship with money was crap. I knew what to do but my beliefs were inhibiting me from anything but success with money. So, I started with writing a letter to money per Peta Kelly's suggestion.

Dear Money,

I am SO sorry that I abused you for so long. I never saw you as anything but something that just got me stuff but never actually filled a need. I used you. I abused you. I took you for granted. Please forgive me. I didn't know what you are capable of. I ignored you thinking that you would still just show up anyway. I promise to do better. To pay attention. To nurture our relationship.

I appreciate you still hanging around after all this. You see as a child I learned that it was easy to make money but super hard to keep. I never saw anyone budget or tell their money where to go as this is rare in the society that we live in. I will communicate with you in a way that is aligned for both of us.

I look forward to strengthening this relationship and the harmony and abundance we will create together.

XO
Becca

I went out and created a budget. But not the one the experts tell you to create. I build what I wanted to spend – not what I made and then distributed it. It made me feel feelings of lack. Every month I started to budget MORE than I was projected to bring in. I connected every morning and asked for guidance on what I needed to do and got aligned with my new found feeling of abundance with my relationship with money. I felt more secure with money. Knowing where it was going and keeping track of when I paid bills and spent money.

I started to practice gratitude for ALL my bills and purchased I make even when the money wasn't there already. I learned respect. I rewrote my story about debt – that it wasn't shameful or bad. It was a choice. A choice to pay for somethings over time. My student loans were a choice to have an experience and pay for it over time. There is nothing good or bad – it is the meaning we give it. Shift your energy into gratitude and watch abundance roll to you.

Months later after creating a plan for my money to flow each month and staying awake to my beliefs and mindset around money I was running into a trauma trigger. This constant fear of running out of money. I have more money know that I EVER have and feel WAY more lack.

It is like the person that wins the lottery that wasn't good with the energy of money prior to winning and blows it all within the first couple years. You don't get money and then get good at it. You get good at monitoring and shifting the energy now and then the money comes in and you hold and increase that vibration.

SO... let's walk confidently through this process. Sit up straight (for real – do it), shoulders back, smile on your face.... (don't pretend – smile already.) I am getting you into the confident energy of stepping into abundance.

It is a FEELING. Forget about the pieces of paper with dead people's pictures on it. You don't ACTUALLY want that. You want how you believe it will make you feel. Abundant. Freedom. Peace.
Let's start to feel these feeling now. Tap in. Take a deep breath and look for areas of your life where you already feel these things. Now stay focused here. ONLY seeing these. When you see something on the contrary. Turn your cheek. Do not give it ANY attention. As what you focus on magnifies quickly. Your FOCUS determines your success.

You want to be successful right?

Focus.

Now journal this:

What you BELIEVE about money.

Write it ALL out.

Now take a good long look WITHOUT judgement at these beliefs. Are any of them coming from a place of lack?

 For example: Money doesn't grow on trees. LACK.
Now re-write ALL the beliefs that come from lack into a statement of abundance.
Instead: Money comes into my life easily and effortlessly.
How about – If I work hard, I will have the money I desire.
Do you REALLY want to work hard for it?
What if it came super flowy and easy?
Would you not be worthy of it? (If your answer is no – worthiness is blocking your desires).
Dive deeper into worthiness if you need to.
Re-write: It is easy for me to make money. It is easy for me to save money.
Managing money is easy for me. My relationship with money is health.
I am incredible with money. I AM a trust fund baby of the universe.

Now this doesn't mean adopt these beliefs and go sit on the couch and watch all the episodes of Suits on Netflix. Although they are very good. It is up to us to take ALIGNED action. Every. Day. Checking in. Soul what would you have me do? How would this look? How can I feel more abundant today? What am I grateful for? How can I foster a deeper feeling of gratitude?

The consistently is in of monitoring our vibration. Staying present. Being aware of our thoughts. Trusting our guidance. Self-care. Self-love. Self-acceptance.
 You are worthy of being, having, and doing it all. You are worthy of the abundance you desire. Will you let it flow through a spicket hose or straight from the ocean? Only you can decide.

Additional journal work:

- In a perfect world (which it is) how would you desire money to show up in your life. Use this as a guideline. Continually see yourself here. FEEL it. Adopt the attitudes, behaviors, and beliefs of being here and watch your life take shape in the way you desire.

- What needs to go?

- What needs to stay?

- What am I no longer available for to increase my abundance in my life?

- Where does money feel uncomfortable for me?

- What stories am I telling about money that I REALLY don't want to happen or continue to happen? How can I re-write these to serve me and my desires?

Bonus: Deep Inner Work

If you are ready to go deeper – I will share with you my process to work through and my daily routine. How I show up in the world. What I do behind the scenes. How I walk each one of my private clients through to SHIFT.
Are you ready?

"The most powerful words in the universe, are ones you use to talk to yourself." Karen Salmansohn

Knowing WHO you are. What lights you up? What can you not stop thinking about? What can you not stop talking about? What did you used to enjoy that you stopped doing due to 'LIFE'? Why did you love it?

Continually create what it is you desire on paper and allow it to change even on a daily basis.

Once you have it all written out. Ask for guidance. Whether you use the cards, journaling, praying - however you receive your guidance best. You could play with each of these to see as I use all of them depending on what feels best.

Do the work. The inspired guidance. The written guidance. Show up. Don't procrastinate.

Decide that what you desire is for you. Work through the doubt as if you are human – you will feel the doubt from time to time. WE ALL doubt ourselves. You are no different.

Stand up with confident energy and do the thing. Send the vibrant energy out in advance of what you are doing. Visualize how you want it to go in advance. KNOW you can do it. KNOW you are powerful.

Hit SUPER FLOW.

TRUST that the universe has your back. That all you desire is already yours. That it is alignment that creates an amazing life – not effort and sweat.

YOUR JOB IS FEELING GOOD. Keep your vibration high!

Lean on YOU. Fulfill your own needs. But also write the story of how you want life to go externally. Script out the feeling. Bring into life your thoughts and beliefs. ENJOY this journey called life. There is no THERE. Experience it all.

Love note for YOU:

Walk YOUR path.

No need to pay attention to anyone else's.

Lean into what feels good to you.

Your truth.

Open your heart a bit more.

Feel more.

Honor your journey.

Decide to flow.

xo Becca

My last love note to YOU.

My life feels complete finishing this book. It started years ago in a hotel in Washington. I was just feeling called to write. It was scary. Letting out many of my deepest feelings of some big lessons of my life. Then I was still super concerned about what others thought of me. How would they judge me once they read this? It has been an incredible ride. Considerably healing. I am grateful for this experience.

I am grateful to YOU for picking up this book. Walking through my processes and doing what resonates most with you. I wish you a life of transformation. I wish you a bright internal light that burns so brightly that you light the way for those walking the path with you and around you. I wish for you to inspire the world with a magical presence. Your authentic self. I wish for you to allow yourself to be seen. To step out behind the curtain and let the world REALLY see you. All of you.

It is then where you will find the freedom and joy you have been searching for. Your soul will sing. The world will rejoice. You will touch the souls you are meant to. You will do what it is you came here to do.

Cheers to awakening your spiritual self.

XO
Becca

About the Author

Becca Grabinski, a midwestern gal on a mission to understand herself, why she is here, what is her purpose, and finding incredible alignment discovered a life changing gift. The gift of pain. She learned what could have been a lifelong lesson of seeing life with the light shining on it. She chooses to walk through the darkness when she couldn't see a thing and take steps on a set of stairs that were not in existence until she stepped. She decided there must be more to life than this.

She has studied under some of the greatest teachers: Tony Robbins, Bob Proctor, Gabby Bernstein, and many more... She put down all the ego and allowed her soul to shine. Raw, authentic, real self to show to the world. There are no accolades, accomplishments, etc. that describe who she is. She is a hope dealer. Here to be a messenger for those that desire transformation. Purpose. Fulfillment.

She currently resides in Minnesota with her blended family of six on the lake where she can feel the flow of the water every morning. Reminder her that she is just a wave in the ocean – free flowing.

To follow her work go to www.beccagrabinski.com.

29995104R00085

Made in the USA
Lexington, KY
05 February 2019